Henry S. Stevens

From Cleveland, Ohio, to Brazil, and from South America to

Europe

Henry S. Stevens

From Cleveland, Ohio, to Brazil, and from South America to Europe

ISBN/EAN: 9783337315573

Printed in Europe, USA, Canada, Australia, Japan

Cover: Foto ©Andreas Hilbeck / pixelio.de

More available books at **www.hansebooks.com**

FROM CLEVELAND TO THE BRAZILS.

THE UNITED STATES AND BRAZILIAN STEAMSHIP LINE
—THE PASSENGERS ON THE "SOUTH AMERICA"—WAN-
DERING REBELS—AT THE WEST INDIES—THE RIVER
AMAZON—CLIMATE OF BRAZIL—CITY OF PARA—EVE-
NING IN THE TROPICS—A MIDNIGHT CELEBRATION—
MORNING IN THE TROPICS—A BRAZILIAN MARKET.

PARA, River Amazon. }
Dec. 17, 1865.

EDITORS HERALD :—The United States and Brazilian Mail Steamship
Company's steamer "South America" left New York harbor on the 30th
of November last, with about sixty passengers, bound for St. Thomas,
Para, Pernambuco, and Rio de Janeiro. The importance of a regular line
of steamers between the United States and the Brazils, after having been
advocated to, and urged upon, the respective governments by many
influential persons in both countries, has at last been recognized, and a
company has been subsidized to the amount of about $150,000 from each
government, for a period of ten years. The trip whereof I now speak is
the third that has been made by this line. Two other steamships, the
" Havana" and the " North America," left New York on their regular
sailing days, the 29th of each of the last two preceding months. This
steamer, the "South America," is commodious and comfortable in all
her appointments, with good officers and servants, and well arranged
staterooms, pleasant awnings, and a large smoking and reading room
upon the upper deck. The importance of all these concomitants is fully
realized in a journey of three times the length of that from New York
to Liverpool, and, during which, so many changes of climate occur. Our
Captain, Tinklepaugh, who will be remembered as connected with the
California line so long, is an experienced navigator and a pleasant
gentleman.

Perhaps an inside view into many of our staterooms will interest some
of your readers. We have merchants from the States going to Para, to

Rio, and to the River Plate, to look up old customers and find new ones. We have the Peruvian Minister to Brazil, who has the honor of being my next at the dinner table. Also the United States Consuls to St. Thomas and Para, and some residents of Rio, gentlemen in whose society I find much pleasure and information. We have an indefinite number of German and Portugese gentlemen whose language or business I don't pretend to understand. There are one or two of these latter who do not seem to think cleanliness "akin to Godliness," and who will never do what has been recorded of a certain fastidious Milesian, who sold his last shirt to buy soap with which to wash it. We have ladies and families of officers belonging to our South Atlantic Squadron, going to meet their husbands. All these gather on deck, daily, and form little *coteries* of their own to play whist, chess, &c., *pour passer le temps*, through these long dreamy tropical days. Mr. Wells, of Wells, Fargo & Co., the pioneer expressman, with his family, goes out to Santa Cruz to spend the winter. There is one group to which I wish to call your especial attention. Here are ten patriarchal looking gentlemen, who, with five or six younger ones, go out to Brazil to gain their freedom in a land of slavery; to escape from their old homes in Mississippi and northern Alabama, to go to nearly the last place on the globe where they can hold slaves. From what I learn, the number of southerners who have gone to Brazil, and who are preparing to go, has been under-estimated at the North. These people on board seem to belong to that middle class of farmers, so common in the South—the men who did most of the fighting at the behest of their superiors—who are still beligerent, though confessing to a lost cause. They are all zealous defenders of slavery. They have

"———cherished it long as a holy prize,"
"Bedewed it with tears, and embalmed it with sighs,"

and are now compelled to confess that their plantation theories of human relations are past praying for in the States. Among them is a General and one or two other officers, who have earned their titles by hard fighting. In the recitals of one of them, however, I am led to suspect an unpardonable economy of truth. In conversation with one of the old patriarchs, who had lived in slavery nearly seventy years, and who looked as though he was bound, let us hope, to a country where there is but one master, in whose eyes superior and servitors are alike, I expressed my surprise that he should, at his time of life, leave his old home with its memories and associations, for a country whose language, climate, people and government were entirely new to him. Upon that he said that he had no objection to living under our government, now that the war was over, but he couldn't stay with the "durned white sneaks in Alabama." Rendered into English, this means that these people, having made themselves extremely obnoxious to their Union neighbors, the aforesaid sneaks, by four years of bitter persecution, now that the side of the medal is reversed, were requested to leave the "diggings" or do worse. They took the hint and here they are. I saw many families fleeing from the Kanawha Valley last spring for the same reason.

After crossing the Gulf Stream, we came into the usual north-east trades, and, at the end of six days, saw land at St. Thomas, This is one of the islands belonging to Denmark—St. John and St. Croix being the other two. St. Thomas has a population of about 15,000, with a pleasant little town and fine harbor. It enjoys quite a large trade. We went on shore, dined at the "Hotel de Comercio," mailed our letters home, got some fruits and supplies for a trip of 1600 miles to our next stopping place, and left late in the evening. Stillman Witt, Esq., spent some days here last winter, and made many friends; several kind inquiries were made for him.

We passed Santa Cruz in the night. The next morning we saw the island of Dominica, and Martinique. We were several hours passing the latter, and being to the leeward and quite near, we were blessed with a calm sea and a fine view. The scenery on the island was very enchanting: the shore is scooped out by divers inlets, and embossed with green promontories. The sandy beaches in the tranquil bays we passed were sweetly picturesque, and the sand as smooth as a well-rolled path. A fresh luxuriant verdure crowns the summits of the hills. A richness and variety of vegetation is seen everywhere, except on the collossal pyramid of naked rock, which rises from the ocean on the north, and stands in bare ruggedness, towering over the fruitful scene below.

We passed the town of St. Pierre, with its white houses and red tiles, and its shipping. Farther inland we saw immense sugar canefields with the smoke of the sugar house or distillery curling up to the blue sky.

We passed to the windward of the island of San Lucia, got a glimpse of Barbadoes, and then saw no more land North of the Equator, but steered almost due South for the mouth of the Amazon. On the 13th of December we were off the coast of Cayenne, in Guiana. We saw no land, but from the shoalness of the water, and its discoloration from the river Orinoco, we could not be very far to the windward. Rain clouds intervened, and the tropical showers pelted down the white caps of the ccean into something like submission. We crossed the equator on the 15th, at 11 P. M. The next day we came in sight of "Salinas," when we took a pilot, and went up the river Amazon.

Who, in his youthful days, from school and story books has not heard of the mightiest river in the world ? The mystery of the female Warriors, with their Amazonian Queen, remain such, I have no doubt with many a grown-up child at this day. I had intended, if I saw the Queen, to get a lock of her hair for Capt. David Price.

Here there are too distinctive seasons of the year, the wet and the dry. The wet, or rainy season, commencing the latter part of December and continuing until July, raining, I am informed, more or less every day. The air is sultry and oppressive, with light, variable winds, and most awful thunder. It generally begins to rain about eleven o'clock in the forenoon and continues until nine or ten at night. From that time, and in the early morning, the weather is fine. Just now we are nearly at the end of the dry or windy season, the wind blowing from the Northeast during the day, with a light breeze in the evening. Lightning is frequent in the horizon at night. The sun during the day is very oppressive, thermometer averaging 84° in the shade. The country along the river is low and covered with magnificent forests. The entire province of Para is said to be an almost unbroken forest, with undergrowth of such density as to render a passage utterly impossible, except to the footpaths of the natives. The country, however, is said to be healthy, although intermittent fevers or agues sometimes attack new comers, and the people up the river, who are employed in gathering sarsaparilla, frequently die of it.

The city of Para is about 100 miles above the mouth of the Amazon, in 1 deg. 30 min. S. latitude. It has about 25,000 inhabitants. Although so nearly under the Equator, the city is said to be healthy. There is probably no place that enjoys a greater uniformity of temperature, and where there is so slight a variation in the barometer from day to day.

The river opposite is about nine miles wide, with many islands. The appearance of the city, as we see it from a long way down the river, corresponds to most tropical cities, with its white houses and red tiled roofs. The triple towers of the huge Cathedral loom up above all, and as we approach nearer, we see many other churches, the custom house, palace, arsenal, forts, &c. We cast our anchor in the stream, Saturday afternoon, and, taking a small boat, we landed and stopped over night at the Hotel d'Italia.

The city fronts on the river, but in its rear there is a long shaded walk called the Estrada des Mangabeiras, from the trees of that name with which it is densely shaded. Last night was brilliant with the star light, the

Southern cross stood almost in the zenith. A long walk I took had more loveliness in it than my imagination had ever pictured before. The dark luxuriant foliage, the waving plumes of numerous palm trees, the fragrance of the opening blossoms of many fruit trees and flowers, the blandness of the evening air in contrast with the noon-day sun, are all beyond the power of my unpracticed pen to describe. I walked through many of the principal streets and squares of the city. They are well lighted with gas. There was music and dancing at many of the Casinos, and the balconies of the houses were filled with both sexes enjoying the evening. Soon after midnight we were awakened by a *feu de joie* of music, *vivas*, rockets, bells, Roman candles and bonfires. My companion, knowing I was posted about the customs, wanted to know "what the matter was." I told him, in confidence, that it was all in honor of the god of "fire and water." That he would see the procession during the day, marshalled by au ex-member of the government, named Palmer, so called from a certain species of tall palm of superior quality, and bearing a hard nut, and that his procession would consist of 200 virgins, (more or less,) a band of music, a lot of military, and several little angels with paste board wings, like I had seen in Mexico. He seemed satisfied with this and went to sleep again. We rose early and found it was "St. Lazarus' day in the morning." All this holy clatter was in honor of the anniversary of that saint. The calander is chock full of saints' days. I am told that about one quarter of the year is taken up with them, and they are celebrated with more or less fervor in accordance with their reputation, and the power they have for performing miraculous cures.

I plunged into the woods that skirt the city in the rear, just at sunrise. Around were stately palms and crowds of mangoes, and every where the broad leafed banana. Rays of green and gold flash from the breasts of humming birds; the linnets, or something like them, are hopping from the tamarind tree to the ground again, and again. Reader, it is a "morning in the tropics."

After breakfast I took a stroll down to the river. Along its margin great numbers of the lower class may be seen bathing, *in puris naturalibus*—no ceremonies are observed.

At the principal landing, near the square and market, there is a crowd of canoes, with cargoes of Brazil nuts, cacao, sarsaparilla, cinnamon, tapioca, balsam of copaiba in pots, and fish and fruit of all descriptions. Here are also parrots, macaws, and a variety of gorgeously plumaged birds, and monkeys of all sizes, not so gorgeous. The appearance of the people is peculiar. The native Indians may be seen both in pure blood and in every possible degree of intermixture with the whites and blacks. They occupy every station in society, as merchant, soldier, priest. sailor, or slave. There is a line of steamers belonging to a Brazilian company that leaves twice a month for the upper Amazon and some of its tributaries, a distance of 3,600 miles, nearly as far as from here to Cleveland. I should like that trip. Professor Agassiz is up there now, somewhere. This government furnished him with a steamer. His report will enlighten the world and attract tourists and emigrants. This city of Para will in time be to the great river what Buenos Ayres is to the Plate, and New Orleans to the Mississippi.

You will hear from me from Pernambuco, 1,200 miles further south, if I have anything to say.   H. S. S.

No. 2.

ALONG THE BRAZILIAN COAST—SUNSET IN THE TROPICS PERNAMBUCO—THE IRON-CLAD SQUADRON—A BRAZILIAN TOWN AND ITS BUSINESS—BRAZILIAN RESIDENCES—THE MONITOR MONADNOCK.

PERNAMBUCO, Brazil, Dec. 22, 1865.

EDS. HERALD: We left Para Sunday noon, December 17th, and steamed down the vast river. At its mouth lies the island of Marajo, as large as some of our smaller States. Here are raised immense numbers of cattle. I am informed that the whole island is devoted to that business. The transition from the Amazon to the Ocean was hardly noticed, so wide is the river at its mouth. We steered South by East to Cape Roque, the point that juts out farthest to the eastward of any on the coast of Brazil, and distant about 1000 miles from the Amazon. This point we passed during the Evening of the 21st, and then, changing our course, ran South by West 200 miles farther, to Pernambuco. During the five days we were coming from Para to this place, we sailed over calm seas, beneath a glorious sky, with the air at summer heat, though with more or less sea breeze. The thermometer averaged 79 deg. on board. We had a few rain showers, and when they came up, or left us, nature's kaleidescope seemed to have quicker changes than I ever saw before. The nights were as mild as evenings in heaven. Among the passengers there is fortunately a varied supply of reading matter, and we get through the day in that way—in conversing—(there is always an eternal clatter, among the Portuguese passengers) in playing chess—in watching the sunsets—the foreign vessels that are now and then in sight, and the *catamarans*, or fishing rafts, with their broad lateen sails, skimming over and under the waves all around us in the mornings. Whenever a light breeze springs up in the night the sea looks like a calico pattern, with its phosphorescent white caps, like dots upon the black ground of the Ocean.

Speaking of Natures drop-scenes, the sunsets, there are here panoramic paintings which no pen or pencil can portray. The zenith of blue diminishes in tone down one third of the vault, and then blends into emerald, which descends through a straw tint into brilliant white as it approaches the horizon. Sometimes, portions of the upper and lower boundaries of the sun were hidden by clouds of a deep chocolate hue, edged with silver, lying like broad belts along the horizon—and then, behind, stretching far upwards towards the zenith, like a fan, were streaks of violet, with the upper edges of a rich fawn color. If you want to see all of this, come yourself some fine evening, you will agree with me, I know, that the old solar scene-painter can get up finer pictures here than any where on the globe. The twilight is hardly known as such. We are not yet directly under the sun as he is running the southern line of the elliptic, and consequently we are not in the predicament of the man who lost his shadow, but we are gradually approaching it. The silver "sheen" you read of, seems to glisten more and more as we go southward.

Both day and night I have great pleasure in watching the ocean. The old sayings, "fickle as the waves," and "unstable as water," seem paradoxical to me when I look out upon its wide expanse, and think that it is now what it was when its waves laved the shores of a lifeless world.

As I look upwards at night to the myriads of orbs that shine in such radiance, I cannot help thinking how much more expansive must be the views at sea in the larger planets. In treading the deck some of these grand nights, it is impossible not to feel a relationship between us and the inhabitants of the worlds in sight, and to believe that, at this very moment, travelers from one clime to another are crossing the oceans there. *Quien sabe?*.

At noon, on the 22d, we saw the monastery on the high point of Olinda, one of the suburbs of Pernambuco, and soon came in sight of the city itself. A portion of the Pacific Squadron now on its way around through the straits of Magellan, comprising the Vanderbilt, the Tuscarora, the Powhattan, and the double turretted monitor, Monadnock, had arrived in port an hour or two in advance, and the usual salutes from the forts on shore were flashing over the waters as we passed by them. We were immediately visited by several officers from the Squadron, anxious for papers and letters from home. Among them was Commodore Rogers, Capt. Ridgely, of the Powhattan, and Lieut. Painter, paymaster of the fleet. The latter is brother to John Painter, Esq The Lieutenant and myself took boat and dined at the Hotel d' l'Europe, and took a view of the city, both by day and gas light.

The City of Pernambuco is in 8 deg., 5 min. S. latitude, and with the exception of Bahia and Rio de Janeiro, is the most important sea port of Brazil. It has about 120,000 inhabitants. Its harbor is formed by a singular coral reef, which extends, I am informed, a long distance on the coast. The temperature here is commonly high, more especially during the night, and until nine or ten in the morning. Then the sea breezes begin to rise by degrees, which refresh the atmosphere until sunset. Notwithstanding the heat, the climate is said to be very healthy. The city seems to consist of three divisions, named Recife, San Antonio and Boa Vista. The two first are connected by a splendid iron bridge, which was brought from England. The carriage ways across the bridge are paved with blocks of granite, and the foot ways with large square brick. The iron gas posts and arches are quite ornamental. In general the town seems to be well built. I noticed many lofty white-washed houses with red tiles and plenty of verandahs and windows to admit the cool breezes. I am told that for miles in every direction towards the interior there are comfortable villas, some very extensive, and constructed with considerable taste. It has all the appearance of being a very busy and thriving town. I understand the merchants have made an immense deal of money the past year or two, principally in cotton, which is grown in the interior, and which comes in, sometimes, in larger quantities than there is transportation to take it away. There are a hundred or more vessels in port, mostly foreign.

The city has a peculiar appearance in approaching it from the sea, the land being very low, so that seen from a distance, the buildings seem to stand out of the water. The lofty buildings are seen first, then the shipping, after which the general features of a large town become visible. Most of the foreign firms are located in the Recife division, which is that nearest the sea. In the division of San Antonio we found most of the shop keepers, among them some very fine siores, with goods of English and French manufacture. We visited quite a large book store, where we saw many works with London imprints, and pictures and engravings decidedly French. In this division are large houses and broad streets well lighted with gas ; here are also situated the Governor's residence, the Treasury, the City Hall, and several Convents. I noticed many squares which presented a gay and lively appearance. The division of Boa Vista contains many broad and handsome streets, but in other parts the buildings are very bad, and built in an irregular and straggling manner. In the Recife division there are many houses fronting the waters, six stories high. Generally the first, or ground floor, is occupied by male servants at night, the second furnishes apartments for lodging rooms, the third and forth for counting rooms, offices, &c., the fifth for dining and the sixth for kitchen. The only reason for having a kitchen in the attic was to favor the upward tendency of smoke and effluvia produced by cooking. Water and other articles are carried up on the heads of negro servants.

The town of Olinda, three miles up the coast, and on the bay, is situated on a hill on whose summit is a monastery, which may be seen a great distance off to seaward. Many of the merchants of Pernambuco have seats here. The houses are beautiful white buildings with handsome gardens. From the monastery, the view is one that every stranger should see. The broad bay is seen stretching with regular incurvation of the coast, away to the south, thirty miles to the Cape St. Augustinho. Far out is the green ocean, with its waves crested with foam. You gaze over the city, proud in her wealth and commerce, and below and around a splendid vegetation, where every leaf seems burnished by the radiance of a tropical sun, yet waving in a constant breeze. In looking at Olinda one is at a loss whether to admire most the whitened houses and massive temples, or the luxuriant manguiras, lofty palms, cocoanut and other trees of beautiful foliage, with which these edifices seem to be nearly buried.

The " raft with two cheese boxes" called the "Monadnock," excites much curiosity here. Her name recalls to my mind pleasant reminisences of a visit made to Mount Monadnock (Indian,"Watch Tower,") in New-Hampshire, last summer. This is the first Monitor that has arrived at this port, and we were not surprised to find the dock lined with spectators. She was visited by large numbers of the people during the day. Her officers inform me that she sails splendidly in all kinds of weather, and in one gale they experienced on their way out, she stood it better than her wooden companions. We shall see the Vanderbilt, belonging to the same squadron, at Bahia, 375 miles south, and our next stopping place. The fleet will rendezvous at Rio de Janeiro in about two weeks, when I hope to renew my acquaintance with some of the officers and also to write you about "that which I shall see,"

H.S.S.

No. 3.

BAHIA—AN UP-HILL TOUR—PECULIAR MODE OF CON-
VEYANCE—THE PUBLIC GARDENS—A SPLENDID VIEW
—BAHIA CATHEDRAL—CHRISTMAS ON THE OCEAN—
BRAZILIAN COAST SCENE—ENTERING RIO DE'JANEIRO.

RIO DE JANEIRO, DEC. 27, 1865.

We left the city of Pernambuco about midnight of the 22d, and arrived at San Salvador, or Bahia de Todos Santos (Bay of all the Saints),
on Sunday, the day before Christmas. We had pleasant weather.
The days were quite hot, but the nights were delightful. With the
Southern Cross above us, the brilliant phosphorescent wave crests below
and around, and the cool sea breezes everywhere, we floated on towards
this Christmas eve. As we were approaching the entrance to the harbor,
we saw a large whale pitching along not far from the stern of our ship.
They are said to frequent this port for some peculiar food which abounds
in its waters, and were formerly caught in large numbers. It is said
that the right to these fisheries at one time brought the Government
$30,000 annually. As we entered the immense bay, large enough for all
the fleets in the world, we saw the outline of the white domes and towers
of the second city of the Empire, and a large number of vessels of all
nations at anchor. Our national flag was splendidly represented by the
United States war vessel Vanderbilt, now on its way to the Pacific via
the Straits of Magellan.

The city of Bahia is not only next to Rio de Janeiro in importance but
also in the beauty of its appearance. ' It is a very ancient place compared
with most others in the New World, having been founded in 1535. It is
in 13 deg., South latitude. It is built on the declivity of a very high and
steep hill fronting the bay, about six miles in extent, and containing
130,000 inhabitants. It consists of an upper and a lower town. A party
of us landed by a small boat in the latter, near the Custom House. This
part of the town consists, principally, of one street, nearly four miles long,
in which are located the shops and warehouses. Some of the latter are of
immense size. Around the landing place are hundreds of canoes loaded
with fruit and produce. Here were some of the finest pine apples and
oranges I had yet seen. The several streets that curve upwards to the
Cidade Alto, that portion of the city on the bluffs above, are all well
paved, and thickly lined with tall houses, but are so steep that no wheel
carriages are used. All drayage in the lower town is done on the backs
of negroes, who lay around in the sun, coiled up like so many black
snakes, while waiting for a job. Like the coffee carriers of Rio, they

j

chant their peculiar measure as they go. It is a very difficult task for a
white person to ascend to the upper town under the hot sun. No omnibus
or carriage can be found to accommodate him, but there are large numbers of sedan chairs, or palanquins, called here *Cadeiras*, always ready.
They consist of an arm chair with a cane seat, protected from the heat
and rain by a circular canopy, covering the whole of it, and surmounted
at the top with an oval crest of fanciful design. The canopy is made of
damask, with extravagantly brilliant figures on it, and opens on both sides.
The two bearers elevate their load and march up hill. The charge is
quite moderate. It is as necessary for familes to keep a cadeira or two,
and negroes to bear them, as it is to keep carriages and horses else-
where. Imagine a party of eight "Americanos del Norte," proceeding
up the long, steep ascent, and through the streets of the upper city in
single file, seated in oriental style, and toted by negroes, on a hot Sunday
afternoon in December.

Our cavalcade, or more properly niggercade, was finally halted on one
of the Broadways of the upper city, at the Hotel del' Univers, opposite
a square whereon stands a church, and next to it a large building which I
was informed was the principle theatre of the place. After an excellent
dinner, we again mounted our palanquins, and went forth to see some portions of the city. Our way to the Gardens, or *Passeio Publico*, was through
several fine streets well built up, along which were many pedestrians of
both sexes and all ages, and many people who, like ourselves, preferred the
sedan chair to walking in the sun. The livery of the carriers, and
the gorgeousness of curtaining and ornaments, indicate the rank
and wealth of the family. At the tall arched entrance to the
Passeio we alighted, and immediately found ourselves under the
dense shades of the mangueiras, the lime trees, the bread fruit, the ca-
shew, and numerous other trees of tropical growth. The air was filled
with songs of birds of all kinds. These are kept in large cages, thirty
or forty different varieties in one cage, like Barnum's "happy family."
From the keeper of one of these I obtained the names of a number,
but on looking over the catalogue, I am satisfied it would tire you as
much to read, as it would me to transcribe them. The mango fruit grows
to a large size here, and some of the trees bear it within two feet of the
ground. The natives eat it, but the taste for it is an acquired one. This
public promenade of Bahia is located on the boldest and most commanding height of the whole town, and those who located it—call them hea-
then if you will—were so far civilized, that this principal park has two
splendid water fronts, one of its sides, from its high parapet, overlooking
the Ocean, and the other the Bay, while an iron railing protects the

visitor from the precipice below. The views from this eminence were truly magnificent. The long rows of whitened buildings, interspersed with splendid foliage, curving away downward from the heights to the waters edge, the broad blue sea on the east, and, to the south-west, the wide expanse of the bay, with its circling mountains, and palm crested islands, made up a picture that I shall not soon forget. On our return, we stopped at the Old Cathedral to vespers. This is an immense edifice, superior, I understand, to any church in Brazil. Near the church is the President's Palace, the Archepiscopal Palace, for this is the spiritual capital of the Empire, a seminary, a military hospital, and other public buildings. It is said that the stonework for some of these were cut, finished and numbered in Europe, and imported ready for erection.

On entering the Cathedral we were quite impressed with its vastness and its excess of ornamentation, lighted up with numberless tall wax candles. The priests were intoning the service to the kneeling congregation, which was composed almost entirely of women. As we advanced we were informed that if we went beyond a certain line, we must kneel with the rest. We preferred to stand outside the sacred line. Here we noticed the brilliantly lighted altars, the curiously carved pillars, and ceilings covered over with gilding, and the wealth, beauty and fashion of the Bahians, as represented by the worshipers. The darkly shaded cheek, and darker and flashing eyes of the Brazilian belles, as shown off by the rich gossamer veil, or the graceful folds of the mantilla, attracted, I am afraid, the attention of some of our party away from the litany and the prayers.

We shipped our anchor during the night and ran out into the ocean. Christmas day, with its hallowed memories, its thoughts of home and friends, was ushered in by a brilliant sunshine and a quiet sea. The usual compliments were passed among the passengers at the breakfast table, and then we scattered, to read, talk or write, sometimes to think, "as we sailed." Within two days of our destination, and far away from the frosty robes, whistling winds and drifting snows of your northern winters, we congratulated ourselves on the pleasant passage of nearly six thousand miles, and rendered thanks to the Great Giver of mercies for continued good health and our present safety. Early in the morning of the 27th, we saw Cape Frio, the north-eastern point of land that is always seen about thirty miles at sea in fair weather, in approaching Rio from this direction. The light on its top, looks, at night, like a distant star. On approaching it nearer, it exhibits two distinct summits, one, several hundred feet higher than the other. Beyond this point the inlets along the coast are bordered by lofty masses of granite, irregularly covered with trees. Then we come in sight of the Corcovado, the Gabia, Two Brothers, and other mountains of singular forms, uncouth names, and stupendous altitude, that surround the Bay of Rio de Janerio. Then comes the Sugar Loaf, a much lower rock, of conical shape, with its steepest side to the west. Close at the foot of this mountain lies the passage into the bay. On both sides, as we enter, are solid masses of granite, skirted with forts.

We are just now engaged in packing our baggage, gathering the scattered books and other articles loaned each other, and collecting the odds and ends generally, of the long "bobbin" of a four week's sea voyage. This admonishes me that I must get this letter out of sight from the expected Custom House officers, who are now coming off. However, they tax everything by the pound, and this light reading won't amount to much. II. S. S.

No. 4.

THE BAY OF RIO DE JANEIRO—THE CITY ARRANGEMENT OF STREETS—A COSTLY RESIDENCE—MAGNIFICENT VIEWS—AN EVENING SCENE—THE BRAZILIAN CLIMATE—OFF FOR EUROPE.

RIO DE JANEIRO, JAN. 1, 1866.

We entered this harbor between the Sugar Loaf Mountain and the fort of Santa Cruz, on the afternoon of the 27th of December. All the writers who have attempted a description of this Bay, have failed in giving a correct idea of its extent and beauty. Fletcher says it can't be described ; that the Bay of Naples, and others of noted grandeur, do not compare with it. Of course I shall not attempt it. My impressions, as we came in, and ever since, were singularly vivid, and, I think, appreciative, but unfortunately I haven't the language at hand. Like the boy in the theatre when the finale of the tragedy was approaching, I threw away the peanuts and every other thought and consideration, and looked on. My hotel is located on the Flamingo Bay, where, from my open windows, I renew my acquaintance with my first impressions day and night. The city is in the 23d° South latitude, and contains about 400,000 inhabitants. It lies almost immediately to the left, as you enter the harbor, and as we passed up along its front to our anchorage, we saw the Bays of Suzano, Bota-fogo, Flamingo, Pedro 1st, the Gloria, De Lapis, and San Luzia. These are all incurvtions (within the harbor), upon the shores on which the city lies. This frontage extends along some six miles, and is thickly built upon. The mountains in the center and rear of the city, seem to be holding high carnival, their old heads pointing in every direction. First, as you enter, is the Corcovado mountain, then the Carioca, Santo Rodrigues and Tejuca. These form the back ground, then Pasmado, de Gloria, San Teresa, Castello, San Antonio, Senado, St. Benito, de Conceicao, Providencia, Livermento, Nheco, Mora de Santa Diego, de Paulos Mattos, da Formega, and de Neves. Upon these last sixteen named hills, (more than Rome ever had,) and their ravines, lies the city. The prominent points on the top of these elevations are generally occupied by Convents and Churches, of which there are about forty in the city. Around about the Customhouse, and the long narrow streets of the business parts of the city, all the room is occupied with buildings, but in every direction, just outside, every residence has a large garden and grounds attached. These private gardens, with the two public resorts, called the Passeio Publico, and the Jardin Botanico, are filled with immense varieties of tropical fruit trees, flowers, palms and mangoes, in such variety of splendor that it fairly makes the senses ache to see and smell them. The shores of the bay, on the opposite side, are covered with rich verdure; a number of villages, plantations of all sorts and sizes, and country seats of elegant appearance, surrounded with trees, are visible. Many islands, also inhabited and wooded, diversify the surface of this inland sea. It seems to me there could not be a more delightful residence on the globe than on one of these. In the city proper, especially in the old part, the streets are mostly straight, but narrow and dirty. They are pretty generally furnished with side walks without curb stones, with a water course or gutter in the centre, which is the usual receptacle of sweepings from the houses. The omnibuses and one horse chaises, or tilburies, with which the city abounds, as well as other vehicles, are obliged to go up one street and down another, each corner of a street having a hand painted on it, indicating the direction. The streets leading out of the city, however, are wide, well built up, and paved.

I am stopping at the Hotel d'Estrangeros, three miles from the Custom House and Palace Square, and on the direct route to Botafogo Bay and the Botanical Gardens. There are splendid residences about here.

One, not yet finished, already costing a million and a half dollars, is being built of marble from Italy. It belongs to a large coffee planter of the interior.

There are two railroads into the country, the Mona road to Petropolis, and the Dom Pedro 2d road, to nowheres, about eighty miles. This is named after the present Emperor. They have just completed a tunnel, a mile and a half long, by the aid of American engineering. I can't tell you much about the interior until I see it. Yesterday I went out to Tejuca, about nine miles. This was accomplished on a railroad, which was formerly a horse or mule road, but is now run with dummy engines built in England. Each engine takes a large two story car holding a hundred passengers, and another car for the second or lowest class of the shoeless and undressed. Many of your readers will recollect Bennets, where I dined, and Mr. Ginty's beautiful place that I visited. We passed in sight of the Emperor's palace at San Christavao. The flag was flying, indicating that he was at home. He has lately been off to the war with Paraguay. From the Heights of Tejuca there is a fine view of the city and bay. The mildness of the climate, which is here a perpetual spring, renders artificial heat unnecessary, and there are no fire places, except in the kitchens, and consequently very few chimneys. This gives, to a northerner, a very queer appearance to the city, a sort of bald or truncated look.

This is by far the largest mart for the export of Coffee in the world. Besides this important article, the exports consist of sugar, rum, ship timber and other valuable woods, hides, tallow, indigo, and the more precious articles of gold, silver, diamonds, topazes, amethysts, tourmalines, chrysoberyls, aqua marinas, etc.

Late in the day, I took a ride along the aqueduct which conveys water to the city from the Corcovado mountains. Here is a view, or a series of views, the most magnificent that can be conceived. The city is before and underneath you, on one side every variety of hill and dale, covered with the most luxurious vegetation, and studded at intervals with the beautiful country residences of the merchants. Beyond, the range of mountains tower towards the sky. The entrance to the harbor is distinctly marked by the Sugar Loaf hill; the white fortifications are perched upon the heights around. The men of war just hauling down their colors, the music of their bands as they salute the departing day, wafted towards you by the last faint puffs of the sea breeze. All these objects, softened by the distance, and illuminated by the glowing tints of the setting sun, complete a picture which cannot be excelled. It is most interesting, at the close of the day, to watch the plants folding up their leaves, and drooping their heads, as if wearied by the heat of the sun. I do not remember ever having noticed the sleep of plants so distinctly as here. The change in the aspect of the leaves is remarkable. The acacias were completely shut up, which is said to increase the fragrance of the flowers. The cassias were folding and reclining. The liquorice pea was, indeed, asleep, and the whole effect of the garden was different from that when I passed up, when the sun was upon it.

I have already seen enough to warrant my belief in the statement that Brazil enjoys one of the finest climates on the globe. Its great characteristic, as compared with other countries, is the general equability of its climate, which constitutes, in fact, the chief element of its salubrity. Even in the height of summer the heat is rarely found oppressive to the North American, and the nights are almost invariably serene and beautiful. In the Northern and Central Provinces, I understand, there is not much dew, so that the delightful coolness of a tropical moonlight may be enjoyed undisturbed by visions of fever and malaria. I am told, by an European sojourner, that years can never entirely efface from his recollection the buoyancy of spirit, unclouded mind, and exquisite appreciation of mere animal existence, which marked the first years of his residence in Brazil. These vivid sensations may be in part determined by the novelty and splendor of a new world, its brilliant skies, perpetual verdure, and the variety, luxuriance and beauty of its vegetable life. The medal unfortunately has its reverse. This favorable condition of the animal economy proves, as in vegetable life, under similar circumstances, but of limited duration, and from seven to ten years, I am told, may be set down as the average period at which a tropical residence begins to affect a Northern constitution to such an extent as to injure the health: the precise epoch being determined, of course, by the constitution, occupation and habits of the individual; which three items, I may add, go far towards making up any individual statistics of longevity, no matter where on the globe he may live. But this country, I think, may be well designated the Italy of the New World, and I am sorry I cannot tell you more about it. It is impossible, as you are aware, to give, within the limits of a gossipping newspaper letter, all one's ideas, impressions and minute information concerning a large city and Empire.

This fact impresses me strongly when I look over a large amount of notes already taken, and which I cannot use for want of time and your space. Therefore I must now close these imperfect sketches of a journey from Cleveland to the land of the Southern Cross, the Cocoa and the

Palm. My business requires me to go home by the way of Europe. I shall leave the French steamer at Lisbon, and go through Portugal to Madrid, thence to Paris and London. I may find leisure during the trip to tell you something about it. I am indebted to Mr. Fletcher's book for some information, to many people at the place I have stopped for kind civilities, and to your readers for their patience.

H. S .S.

No. 5.

FROM SOUTH AMERICA TO EUROPE.

RIO DE JANEIRO—PICTURESQUE FEATURES—PUBLIC CONVEYANCES—POLICE REGULATIONS—BRAZILIAN WOMEN--MODE OF SHOPPING—FEATHER FLOWERS— A BRAZILIAN RAILROAD--A BIG TUNNEL.

Rio de Janeiro, Jan. 9, 1866.

We had a fellow passenger on the "South America," coming out, who had the infelicity of reading one of my former letters to you, in manuscript, and, a regular old Fadladeen in criticism, he cautioned me not to use the personal pronoun too much. I may possibly offend good taste, in your opinion, in this respect, but the old adage says, "He who runs may write to those who run, to read," and, as I propose to let nothing go unseen for the lack of being looked after personally, I don't see how I can help it in writing this veritable history of my journey. After all, there are men in the world to write about, as well as hemispheres, empires and cities. Scenery, without people, is pretty much what a panorama is compared to a play.

On the afternoon of our arrival at Rio, after committing our baggage to the tender mercies of the custom-house officers, we took a launch for the *Largo de Paco*, (Palace Square). Here the boatman brought us safely, charged us mercifully, and bade us "go with God." The hack-men crowded around us pretty much as they do in civilized countries, and we made our way into one of their vehicles. The Hotel do los Es-trangeros is located about three miles from the landing, on the *Ponte de Catette*, Flamingo Bay. The street of Botafogo commences here, and extends about a mile further. The streets of the city, along the whole four miles to the latter place, are lined with shops, dwellings, and churches, with mazes of curved cross streets, also densely populated. The Hotel is quite an extensive affair, with long gardens extending back to the shores of the bay. The surf]rolls up on the beach, affording us a pleasant bath every morning, and a lulling music at night. We chose a room on the third floor, where, from the windows, never closed, we look out on such an extensive and varied view that I am never tired of it. The city, with its snow white buildings, more beautiful from far than near, covering the plains and hill sides, looks splendidly in the evening light. The Sugar Loaf Mountain, at the entrance to the bay at our right, the beautiful bay with the forts on the heights opposite, the distant and dim outline of the Organ Mountains, as seen when the early morning is just bursting into perfect sunlight, make a scene for the memory as well as for the eye.

There are a large number of omnibuses running in all directions to and from the centre of the city. These carry only a certain number, which number is painted on the outside of each vehicle. The conductor is subject to a penalty if more are admitted. The omnibuses are rough vehicles, drawn by four mules, and driven at a tremendous pace in a galloping run, over stone pavements, gutter ways, and any obstacle. If the reader can consider himself, *ceteris paribus*, on the inside of a kettle, and that kettle tied to a frightened dog's tail, he can have an idea of what riding in one of these concerns feels like. For this you pay about twenty cents. Another public vehicle is very much in use here, called a *caleso*, like the Quebec *caleche*, or English tilbury. It is a chaise top on a pair of wheels, whose motive power is a small mule with immense har-ness. This conveys one passenger only, at a charge of one milreis (about 54 cents) from our hotel into the city.

The police here is a semi-military institution, but, at the present time, most of the force is absent, having been sent off to the war with Paraguay last April. The city is now governed by the national guard, made up principally from the negro population. The night police force is com-posed of citizens who are drafted for the purpose, and who are so fond of each other, or afraid of solitude, that you may always see them in squads of three or four. They are never about after midnight, consequently robberies are very frequent.

A charter for a series of street railroads, was obtained some years ago, but for several reasons they have not been built. They are very much needed, and will, when built, revolutionize the local transit, besides proving a profitable business. The streets in the direction of Botafogo bay, and to the Botanical garden, which is six miles distant, are perfectly level, and, after about one-third of the way, are wide enough for a double track. In the business part of the city, the cars would go out one street and return another, parallel to it, as the carriages are obliged to do now. One noticeable peculiarity here is the absence of ladies from these public conveyances in the streets, and at the stores in the city. I have seen but a few in the omnibuses, but when cars are substituted, there will be a very great difference. In a whole day's walk I have not seen a single pretty woman, not a solitary representative of

"La doncella muy fermosa."

I have met, at dinner and dancing parties, some of our fair country women, and quite a number of English and French ladies, but I have not yet seen a really beautiful Brazilian. A Frenchman and an Englishman both assured me they were very scarce, and upon whatever subject you can get these two nationalities to agree, you may consider it as demonstrable as any thing in Euclid.

Ladies are never seen shopping, except in carriages, when the goods are brought out for their inspection. Generally, whatever is required, is sent for, or samples to select from are sent to their houses. The pedlar is a popular institution. He goes from street to street, with his two clapping sticks. with which he gives notice of his approach. A stout negro follows him with his large case of wares on his head. He is always a welcome visitor, and no doubt drives many a profitable bargain. Everything is carried here upon the heads of the negroes. The day after my arrival. I got my trunk from the Custom house, and gave a negro half a dollar to tote it to the Hotel. He trotted off with it on his head, and accomplished the three miles nearly as quick as I did in a tilbury.

Senor G., the engineer of the gas works, told me that when he first came here, he put a gang of twenty negroes to work filling up a ditch with broken stone, and furnished them with the like number of wheelbarrows. Looking soon after from his office window, he saw them hard at work, each with his wheelbarrow on his head !

Speaking of shops, the Rua do Ovidor, the Broadway of Rio, which is about twenty feet in width, contains many fine collections of goods, mostly French. Another long street is almost entirely devoted to the gold workers and their *brilliantes*. Another is given over to harness and leather work, and around the corner is the principal meat street, where all kinds of *carne* can be bought. I visited many of the shops where the beautiful feather flowers of the country are for sale. Here is a strong temptation to spend your *milreis*. I have sent home some beautiful varieties, including wreaths, and flowers of green and gold made from the breasts of humming birds. The Brazilian beetle, or fire-fly, are set as sleeve buttons, pins, and other articles of jewelry. I made most of my purchases from the wife of a celebrated maker in the Rua Ouvidor, who was lately ordered off to the Amazon by his imperial master, to join the staff of Agassiz, as the taxidimist of the expedition. The finest flowers, however, are to be had at the Convents of Bahia, where I found them much cheaper than in Rio. I accepted an invitation to a dinner, given on the evening of New Year's day, by a wealthy English gentleman, and although the rooms and the table were adorned by some of the rarest and most splendid flowers from his garden, yet my attention was attracted to a large and brilliant boquet upon a stand, which I found was made of delicate feathers, and which our hostess assured me she had purchased fifteen years ago.

The attention of the Imperial Government has been attracted of late years, to the system of railroads as a means of developing the immense resources of the Empire. I had an invitation from a contractor whom I had known in the States, to take a journey into the interior, on the Estrada de Ferro de Don Pedro Segundo—the railroad of Don Pedro 2d.— I accepted the proposition for a dia do campo—a country day—as became a traveler of an inquiring mind, holding good the scrap of philosophy, "to see *what* you can *when* you can." We set off in a tilbury, at six in the morning, for a five miles ride through the city, to the railroad depot. This building is a substantial and convenient structure. The cars are both of the English and American plan, In the train I went on, there were most of the former. These are apartments, opening on the side, containing eight comfortable cane seat arm-chairs. In one of these I saw one of the fairer sex with an infant in her arms. She did not allow the presence of the company to interfere with the conscientious and elaborate performance of her maternal duties, while the men in the same car were puffing their cigars, making, as I passed, a delicate blending of the smoke house and nursery. The apartment assigned us was occupied by my friend, Mr. Humbert, the contractor for the big tunnel, his son and family, and ourselves. The road runs for some miles past suburban villas, almost buried in the redundant foliage of their splendid gardens. About three miles out, we arrived at the Emperor's private station, located on the grounds of his palace of San Chistovao. These grounds are very extensive and beautiful. In the long shaded aisles of walks and drives, the deep green arches are so massive that the fountains have scarcely light enough to dance in. The road passes directly along their whole length for nearly a league. with many views of the palace itself. We soon left all traces of city life behind us. and got into the regions of the large coffee estates. Here we see the houses of the wealthy planters and the coffee trees in thousands. Occasionally we pass corn, sugar and tobacco fields. There are about ten or twelve stations in the fifty-seven miles we went, but ours, being *par excellence*, the express train, but four stops were made. At the end of forty miles, through a rolling, cultivated country, we came to the ascent of the mountain. Here the lamps are all lighted in the carriages, for we have sixteen tunnels to go through, of more or less length. The g ..le for seventeen miles is an average of ninety-five feet in the mile. On he top, therefore, we are about seventeen hundred feet above the p ...ns. The road winds around very much, affording magnificent mountain views, and giving abundant evidence of a splendid success in engineering. At one point we look across a valley a thousand feet deep, and there, high up above us, is the road, hanging on the edges of the opposite mountain range, and while it cannot be a mile across, we are to travel eight miles before we reach it. The great tunnel has but just been completed. It is the last one, and there the road begins to descend. Beyond, the road is finished thirty miles further. It is intended to reach Rio S. Francisco, about two hundred miles altogether. This tunnel is one and a half miles in length, with four shafts of immense depth. There, for seven long years, have my Maryland friend and his son labored faithfully and well. The Emperor visited it the other day, and pronounced it good. The work has therefore been accepted, and the contractor complimented for his skill and perseverance under very trying difficulties. He goes home in the spring, via Europe, where he has three children at school. I have promised to call and see them in Paris next month. At the station just beyond the tunnel, called Mendes, we alighted and took mules for a zigzag road of two miles in length, up the mountain and directly over the tunnel and near the main shaft. Here lived our host on what had formerly been a coffee estate. As we rode up to the gate. I was escorted by a son of my old friend, Mr. Carleton, of Cumberland, whom I had not seen for a long time. "What, not another acquaintance?" said my fellow traveler, as we alighted from the mules ; "I had supposed," said he, "that here, on the top of a mountain, in the interior of Brazil, six thousand miles from home, you might afford to be unknown." I reminded him that the world was growing smaller now-a-days, and that American traveling nature abhors a vacuum. "We shall find them wherever we go."

The health of this place must be perfect. Its elevation above the plains, fine mountain air and water, and equable climate, always spring, has made it noted for its salubrity. The mere breathing the air is a luxury. We spent here six most delightful hours. The good dinner was relished. We had mountain kid, roasted, and all kinds of vegetables and fruits from the gardens. We left our friends reluctantly, declining to stay over night, as we had business engagements next morning. Both in going and returning, we could not help remarking upon the solidity and permanency of the construction of the road in every particular. I have seen no better road yet, in these respects. It was commenced by an English company years ago, but was finally taken by the government and finished by Americans. The last Engineer is Maj. Ellison, who is from Massachusetts, to whom great praise is awarded by every body.

We arrived at our hotel in the evening, and slept soundly that night, notwithstanding the noise of two casuistic cats somewhere on our tiled roof, after as pleasant a day as I remember to have spent. Let him who can find anything much pleasanter, go his ways and make the most of it.

And now I must terminate this already too long letter. I find I cannot condense an Empire into a paragraph, and will therefore give of what occurred during my few remaining days' stay, in another letter, which I will write on the steamer, and mail at Lisbon or Madrid. H. S. S.

No. 6.

RIO DE JANEIRO AGAIN--THE U. S. PACIFIC SQUADRON
--IMPERIAL VISIT TO THE MONADNOCK—THE EMPE-
ROR AND HIS FAMILY—ANOTHER DAY AT TEJUCA—
THE GAS WORKS--WATER WORKS—AMUSEMENT.

CAPE DE VERDE ISLES, Jan. 23, 1866.

The arrival of our splendid Pacific squadron, with the ugly looking
Monitor "Monadnock," was the event of the last week of my stay at Rio
de Janeiro. The echoes of the immense guns of the armament as they
saluted the forts and war ships in the harbor, wakened up the lazy Bra-
zilians. and set the carping Britishers to thinking. These latter don't
like to have the old eagle scream so close to their ears. During the last
four years, the large English population have, with scarcely an exception,
exulted in our every defeat, and ridiculed our cause in every way, The
few loyal Americans, in doubt as to the result of the struggle, were brow
beaten, and in many instances openly abused by the English. But it is
their turn now. They feel as did the Greeks at the dawn of Salamis.
American stock went up on this arrival. The few self-expatriated countrymen of ours, who left their country and their negroes for the good of
both, look upon this manifestation of our naval power with a regretful
sadness. 'It makes them a little homesick. Early on a beautiful morning the fleet sailed proudly into the splendid bay, and at the first pop of
the guns I was at the window overlooking the entrance to the harbor, the
Sugar Loaf mountain, and the opposite fortifications. The peculiar thrill
which always accompanies the sight of the old flag in foreign ports, was
intensified by the magnificence of the panoramic show. Such things
startle me now and then, as I suppose the strange melody would have
done, coming as unexpectedly, when the first sunbeams fell on Memnon's
statue. We danced in costume du nuit, tried to sing the "Star Spangled
Banner," dressed, and went out into the city.

The last day of our stay at Rio, was appointed by the Emperor to visit
the monitor. He had never seen one. With his son-in-law, Comte d'Eu
and attendants, he started from the dock at 11 o'clock. We had received
an invitation from Lieutenant Painter to go on board the Tuscarawas
which was lying near the monitor, and were pulled off in an eight-oared
boat at about the same time. The day was lovely, and as we came along

side, we were honored by a salute of twenty-one guns from the Vanderbilt, Powhattan, Tuscarawas, Kansas and Junietta, and immediately the
boys in blue commenced running up the rigging of the different vessels,
to man the yards. As we were gracefully removing our hats to acknowledge the civility, we saw the Emperor's yatch stop at the side of the
Monitor, near by, and the august party went on board. We conceded to
him a fair share of the ovation, and went on board the Tuscarawas, where
we had a good view and a nice lunch.

We afterwards rowed over to the fort of Santa Cruz. Through ignorance
of its necessity, we had no permit, and could not enter and examine the
works. Not being, any of us, military men, which, in a company of three,
from our land of Brigadiers, was quite a wonder, we persuaded ourselves
we had not lost much, for from the base of the fortress we had a charming
view of the White City, the harbor, with its gay banners streaming, the
green valleys running up into the gorges of the hills, and the sea rolling
as far as the eye could reach. As we rowed back under the lee of the
huge fifteen inch guns of the monitor, we were consoled by the reflec-
tion that one blaze from her would knock the old fort into a cocked hat.

We did not get a very near view of the Imperial party this time, but,
the other day, as I was sitting in front of a cafe in the Rua Dericta, the
sound of bugles and the tramp of horsemen announced the approach of
his Majesty, who rode past in his usual galloping style, in a carriage with
the Empress, escorted by a troop of cavalry and several outriders in gay
costume. It was a Saint's day, and he had come into the city, to attend
service at the Carmelite Church, near the Largo do Paco. Hither we
went for the same purpose. The aisles, which I had seen all lonely the
day before, were crowded with zealous worshippers. The high altar was
blazing with a multitude of soft lights. The ceremonial vestments were
very rich. An orchestra aided the organ, for here they always have wind
instruments, and violins and drums in their choirs. High over all, the
morning sun streamed through the painted windows, and you could see
the incense, which was burning near the altar, curling around the capi-
tals and clinging to the gilded arches. Near the altar, and under a canopy of what seemed to be old pennons, on a raised seat, sat the Emperor
Don Pedro 2d. The services lasted about forty minutes. I stood directly behind the line of halberdiers that formed in the principal aisle of
the church, and, being a trifle taller than the soldiers, his Majesty had a
good view of me as he passed, bowing along out. Don Pedro has the
reputation of being a fine scholar, good linguist, and a pleasant gentleman. He is related by blood and marriage to nearly all the crowned
heads of Europe. He has a good countenance, and a fine commanding

figure, being some three or four inches over six feet in height. His two daughters were married some two years ago; one, the heir apparent to the throne, to the Comte d' Eu, grandson of Louis Phillipe, and the other to the Duke Saxe. The Comte has a residence in the Languieras, near where I stopped, and I have met him several times. They are both said to be clever young men. The Empress is two years older than her husband, and looks exactly like her photographs.

On the Saturday previous to our leaving Rio, we were invited to visit Tejuca again, and accordingly left in the 1–30 P. M. train. The mansion of our host is located on a plateau of one of the numerous elevations that abound in that region, with a fine mountain air and views of the ocean. It rejoices in one of the most delightful *patios* I had seen, filled with orange and lemon trees and fragrant flowers. From the terraced gardens which slope off down to the edges of precipices a perfect range of wooded glens can be seen, crossing and recrossing each other. The fig, red lucerne, and pomegranate, grow luxuriantly beneath the tall palm. The wild mountain torrents are seen dashing down the opposite cliffs and are heard, brawling and fretting, over rocks far down below, on their way to the ocean. It was a scene that at once combined tropical luxuriance with the summer freshness of our mountain views. This combination of landscapes will win one thoroughly from all other scenery after a time. At first, the eye looks in vain for the blended shadows of Northern landscape, and the rustic character so suggestive of country life, but in its clear distinctness, its marvellous beauty of outline, and in that vastness of view imparted by an atmosphere of such purity, there are indisputable charms. However, there may be persons of a different opinion; I only give mine, and am sometimes grieved in my own heart to acknowledge how little I can catch of a connoisseur's enthusiasm,—wondering within myself wherefore I could not feel like that other man, whose raptures I have listened to—and with sore misgivings that some nice sense has been omitted in my nature : wonderfully painful things are these little appeals to an inner consciousness. I know also that there is a wide difference between admiring what is beautiful yourself, and so portraying it that others may endorse your taste. A wise man was the learned Judge who refused to give reasons for his judgment. He said, "The opinion may be very good, but the reasons quite the contrary." At the dinner table we met some eighteen or twenty English ladies and gentlemen, among them the British Consul and family. After that was over I wandered around the grounds and over the hills until the moon came up.

The stars twinkled busily—undimmed, it seemed to me, even by the flood of light which was over all things. The rest of the picture was in slumber, from the broad unrippled sea to the heavy turretted mountains that went step-wise towards the sky. It was a night of all others to take the fairies out to dance. We had music and dancing after supper, and retired in good humor with every body and the rest of mankind. Of a certainty it is a wise thing to send invalids to the mountains of Tejuca.

I spent part of a day at the Gas Works. These are owned by an English company, have proved valuable property, and are very extensive, covering several acres of ground. The manufacture of all kinds of pipe, gas fittings and fixtures, lamps, chandeliers, bronze work of fine descriptions, are carried on by the company, there being no trade of the kind in the city. They are obliged to keep on hand an immense lot of large lanterns for use during illuminations, of which these people are very fond. The last one was on the occasion of the Emperor's return, a short time since, from the war with Paraguay. Most of the employees are slaves. There were about twenty negro boys, belonging to the Emperor, at work on fine bronzes and brasses. I was informed that they learned the trade readily and made good workmen. The lamp posts in the city are placed very much nearer each other than ours are, and extend for miles in every direction. We found them at Tejuca nine miles out. The company have 124 miles of gas mains, and 5,800 public lights, ten hours each night. For this they receive 108 milreis, cash, per annum, which amounts to the nice little sum of $348.256 00 in the aggregate. This is paid by Government and not by the city, as with us. They use a superior kind of English cannel coal which costs them here about $15 per ton. The gas is of the first quality. The charge to private consumers is $4 per thousand in specie. Instead of lime, they use a kind of red earth which is obtained by hauling, and is inexpensive. This contains peroxide of iron, alumen, argillaceous matter, &c. People bring their children here to be cured of the whooping cough. The carriages of the Prussian Minister was at the door with three of his children who had been inhaling over the purifier while it was being cleansed out. The gas works at Bahia, Pernambuco, Para, Buenos Ayres, and Monte Video, are all owned by the English, and are managed pretty much the same.

The city is well watered as well as lighted. An aqueduct from the Corcovado, and one from Tejuca, in a different direction, give a bountiful supply. At almost every corner there are huge brass cocks in the walls, about five feet high, and, underneath, a stone block to rest the vessel upon. Here the slaves and servants may be seen at all hours of the day drawing water in calabashes, buckets, earthen jars, &c., and going away with them on their heads. This is also a government expense, there being no direct tax for anything, not even for making sewers or paving streets. It all comes out of the whole country, through taxes on imports and from other sources of revenue. It is as if the city of Newburg should be taxed for lighting and paving the streets of the village of Cleveland.

Of the Courts of Justice I cannot say anything, as, fortunately, I had no business with them. I happened by a magistrate's office one day and just stepped in a moment. It was a case of dog, and, as I had seen the same thing several times at home, I left.

Of their school system, I refer you to Fletcher, who has considerable to say on the subject. Some of the Collegiate buildings and grounds are very fine, the one at Botafogo, for instance. They are all Catholic.

I was so busy while at Rio that I did not attend any of the several places of public amusement in the evenings. My companion, however, went once with some officers of the Tuscarawas, to the *Alcazar*, where, among other things there was a ballet performance. He says the gyrations and saltations were about the same as we see at home, only more so. I expect to see some of these dances In Spain, when the reader, if it so pleases him, shall hear more of them. Most of the dancers here are imported from Seville and Cordova. We have an *Impresari* on board our steamer who is going there to bring out a lot to the cities on the river Plate, where he has theatres.

My next letter, for I take it for granted that you have had enough of this, will be dated from somewhere else.   H. S. S.

No. 7.

BAHIA—AN ITEM ABOUT CATHEDRALS—OFF FOR ST.
VINCENT—OUR COMPANY—READING THE PRESIDENT'S
MESSAGE—HOW THE DAYS ARE SPENT—ST. VINCENT—
ENTERING THE TAGUS.

LISBON, Jan. 30, 1866.

On the morning of January 9th we shipped from Rio, for this port, via
Bahia, Pernambuco and Cape de Verde Islands, in Her Majesty's Royal
Mail Steam Packet "Oneida," which runs between Rio and Southampton,
England. This is a powerful iron screw steamer, built for, and originally
run in, the Australian trade. There were the usual crowds on the docks
and on board, to see their friends off, with waving of handkerchiefs and
drying of tears, It is hard to be disinterested spectators of kissings at
such partings, where the brightness of the eyes and the freshness of the
lips give such enlarged and delightful ideas of the philosophy of adapta-
tion. But a traveler, who is but a rolling stone, can expect to gather no
such moss.

Steamers are no picturesque tourists, and we ploughed along at the
rate of ten miles the hour, passing under the lee of the Vanderbilt, Ju-
niata and the Monitor, through and among the shipping, including some
fifteen ex-blockade runners, who were at anchor. Onward we went, out
into the Southern Ocean, for a transatlantic trip of three weeks duration.
This ship has proved herself a good sea vessel in every respect, but her
passenger accommodations do not compare with some of our sea-going
steamers. The people on board, as is usual, represent various nationalities, the English, in this case, predominating. We are already intimately
acquainted with many of these latter, by virtue of being thrown together
on the quarter deck to seek amusements and conversations. Strange
indeed, is this kind of traveling acquaintanceship, familar without friend-
ship, frank without being cordial. I have often thought what curious
pictures of life might be thrown accidentally together, in steamships
railroads and watering places. How free is all the intercourse of those
who never expect to meet again! always making up little cliques to be
dissolved in a day—actually living on the eventualities of the hour
for their confidences, the oddities of this one, the eccentricities of that,
politics, the weather, &c., forming the basis of talk.

I will not trespass upon your readers patience by giving minute de-
criptions of characters I might introduce. In this era of universal vaga-

bondage, no charities are wasted upon our estimate of each other in traveling, and, besides, prominent traits of character lie so lightly on the surface that they are capable of but little elucidation. Next in numbers to the English on board, we have many of that race who, with all the odds of a great majority against them, enjoy a marvellous share of this world's prosperity. You may know them by a certain aquiline character of nose, and a peculiar dull lustre of the eye. They have "smelt the battle from afar off," and can tell you all about Paraguay and her troubles, As for the balance of our passengers, with the exception of a confederate Colonel and an American, they might all be called "cognate numbers," and I don't intend to trouble you with them. The rebel Colonel was formerly on Stonewall Jackson's staff, but afterwards went into the blockade running trade, and has made many successful trips. The object of his visit to Brazil was to dispose of several of the blockade runners. There are now fifte n in the harbor of Rio. Several of them have been sold to the governm.nt for transports. The Colonel is a fair specimen of his class. We have been together quite often, on board and on shore, and we do not hear a word about the past from him. It is so sorry a subject that I have seen no rebel officer yet, but who will deprecate a discussion on what has happened. There is one marked peculiarity among them all, and that is their hatred of the English. How I would like to be able to sketch the scene on the quarter deck after we left Pernambuco, where we obtained a London paper which contained our President's message. The group consisted of three Americans, our Colonel, and about twenty Englishmen, many of whom were highly intelligent gentlemen. The Colonel was called upon to read the message aloud for the benefit of all. This he did, emphasizing certain passages, especially that one about England. One young Englishman ventured to say that there was no use talking about indemnity, "Lord Russell had written his last letter," &c. The Colonel fired up in his style, and offered to stake his life that if the United States demanded payment, flat footed, with war as the alternative, England would pay at once. This brought on quite a scene among us, in which lively words were passed.

We went on shore at Bahia, where we arrived in four days from Rio. Here I had a better opportunity of seeing the public gardens and churches than before. We landed at the Market Place. No body ever starved to death, I take it for granted, in Bahia. I saw no preparations for anything of the sort while I was there. I visited the Cathedral, the largest in the Empire. I have seen most of the churches in Rio, but this one excels them all in that peculiar solemnity of grandeur which makes the Gothic the architecture of religion. As we entered, many of the windows were shaded, and it was some time before our eyes, fresh from the glare of the pavements, became sufficiently accustomed to the gloom, But, by degrees, the fine galleries, the gorgeous glass, the simple and lofty arches in concentering clusters, the light columns of the altar screen and the perfect fretwork of the choir, grew into what might be called bewildering distinctness. Here were several worshippers on their knees.— I went into a church at Rio the other evening just at dark. A few candles were lighted upon a single altar,' and a priest was kneeling before it reading some prayers, to which a few school boys were responding in that peculiar caterwaul so characteristic of these scholastic devotional exercises. With this exception, and that of a few poor people upon their knees in quite audible prayer, darkness and silence had the church to themselves, and our echoing footsteps, the dim glimpses of arch and column and cornice, the shadowy high altar and gloomy choir, gave semblance of awe to this huge building which it wanted very much in the daylight.

The freedom of access peculiar to all these churches has a real value, so it seems to me. A thousand unworthy motives may attract people to the stated service, while sorrow, poverty and shame may drive away from public observation those who need the consolations of religion most. How proper is it, then, that there should always be a place of refuge open for the desolate. How wise and just that all facility should be afforded for that humble, unobtrusive worship which cares not to be seen of men. The grand cathedrals of the middle ages all over the world, might well be called mere monuments of vanity and superstition, were they only opened for a few hours in the week, that well dressed piety might enter and be briefly and respectably devout.

At every city of the Empire I have visited, and especially at Bahia, I have noticed the long rows of shops devoted to the sale of miracle work ing images, from those of the Virgin down to the last Saint in the calen dar. These are all sizes and prices, manufactured of wood, metal and clay. In these spiritual drug shops, there is a large trade driven for money. This, and other customs, and the general bad reputation of the monks and priests, seems to require the attrition arising from the presence of other creeds and sects to keep them up to the professed standard of Christian purity. This no doubt accounts for the difference in so many respects between the customs and Clergy here, and those in the States. It is another argument against monopolies.

We arrived at Pernambuco at noon on the 15th of January, and left the same evening. Here we cut loose from the New World and steered a Northeasterly course to Cape de Verde Islands, our next stopping place, and 1,600 miles distant. These islands are off the coast of Senegambia, in Africa, in latitude 17° North.

During the week we were making this distance we had light variable head winds until we struck the South-east trades, when we were able to use sail, which aided our steam some forty miles a day. There was a rain storm or two, but no very heavy sea. We crossed the Equator at 11 P. M. Jan. 17, The Line was not visible to the naked eye, probably owing to the darkness of the night. Our community on board, consisting of some two hundred and forty persons, are very quiet and regular in their habits. Bath at 6:30 A. M. (That is mine, some have different hours.) Coffee served in state-room at 7. Breakfast at 9. Lunch at 12. Dinner at 4. Tea at 7 P. M. Whist, euchre, chess, &c. commence at 8. The lights are all extinguished at 11. We have an amateur dramatic company on board, made up from among the stewards, waiters, &c. From long practice they do very well in their comedies and farces, which are gotten up in the grand dining saloon. The bill is pasted on the usual bulletin board, announcing the play, characters, &c., early in the day. On this board, too, we find the result of the ship's log at 12 o'clock such day for the previous 24 hours. I transcribe two of them, which show the difference in the direction of the wind in its action upon the speed of the vessel, in the two respective days : January 21st, Lat. 11.8 N., Long. 27.12 W. Run 180 miles. To St. Vincent 375 miles. Jan. 22d, Lat. 14.34 N., Long. 25.59 W. Run 219 miles. To St. Vincent 156 miles. On Sundays we have the Episcopal service read on board at 11 A. M., at which there is a general attendance of passengers, officers and crew.

On the morning of the 23d, we sighted the land of San Antonio, one of the Cape de Verde group, and soon passed round into the harbor, a basin, wherein lies the little town of St. Vincent. Why these Islands are called green, I cannot imagine. It has been indisputably demonstrated that the whole bay was originally the mouth of a volcanic crater, and the surface of burnt stone, argilaceous earth, and absence of all vegetation, would seem to verify it.

There being nothing in the town itself, we turned conchologists and went shell gathering around the shores of the bay,

> " Deep in the waves is the coral grove
> Where the purple mullet and the gold-fish rove.''

But here the coral was near the surface, as were some of the mullets. We collected several fine specimens of coral, and some delicate shells.

This place is a convenient harbor for vessels, and is only used as such, and as a depot for coaling. We left at 7 P. M. and passed out into the ocean for a trip of 1550 miles to Lisbon. We passed the Peak of Teneriffe on the coast of Morocco, on the 27th, and now, on this morning, the 30th, just twenty-one days out from Rio, we are passing into the river Tagus,

H. S. S.

⁕

No. 8.

TOUCHING EUROPE—LISBON—A CITY OF EARTHQUAKES CHAPEL OF ST. ROCH—A PORTUGUESE OPERA HOUSE OFF FOR SPAIN—THE CORK FORESTS—SANTAREM—THE SPANISH-PORTUGUESE RUBICON—IN SPAIN—ELVAS— BADAJOZ.

MERIDA, Spain, Jan. 3, 1866.

It may be as well to state to the reader at once, that the same descriptive line, without especial personal adventure, must be adopted by all travelers in the Old World. The ground has been gone over so many hundreds of times by those who have such leisure as to enable them to perfect or elaborate their story, that nothing must be expected from this slight sketch of my subject. But the same feeling occurs to me, that I have no doubt does to the mind of every one who visits the Old World for the first time, that notwithstanding we have studied all the ancient and modern histories, and have read all the " Familiar Letters," "Journals," "Glimpses," "Sketches," "Scribblings," etc., etc., with which the press has been prolific for a century, until our heads are full of a jumble of mountains, palaces, cities, rivers, ruins, plains and people, yet, after all that, we do not realize the thing itself until we see and feel it. I suppose that the almost universal desire to write, while here, is to be mainly attributed to this fact. It seems a new revelation to us, and we must write it out.

My advent into the Old World through ancient Lusitania, now Portugal, was marked by no particular sign. The river Tagus widens out as we approach the city of Lisbon, and there forms a large bay. It was crowded with vessels of all nations. We passed the Fort St. Julien at 7 A. M. on the morning of the 30th of January, then the Castle Belem, and in full view of the palace upon the high grounds in the rear, and then, three miles farther on, to the landing in front of the city. We had heard of the revolution in Spain, at the Cape de Verdes, and were almost deter- mined to avoid it and go to Southampton direct, but the long sea voyage had just been enough of that kind of life, and the tales of recent ship- wrecks and gales in the English Channel, all combined, determined us to try the land for awhile. I wanted to see Spain. It had never occurred to me that I should see, except in dreams, the bright land I had so often seen in them; and now, within so short a distance, I could not avoid the opportunity. The route to London, via Madrid, Bayonne, Bordeaux, and Paris, overland, is but two days longer than by sea to Southampton.

The city of Lisbon is beautifully situated on the northern bank of the Tagus, about six miles above the entrance of the river into the Atlantic. It is built on a succession of hills in the form of an amphitheatre, and is about 9 miles long, with a population estimated at 300,000. The modern portion of the city is very fine and well laid out. The streets are clean, well paved and lighted. This part has replaced the old portion of the city, which was destroyed by the great earthquake of 1755. From the earliest times, Lisbon has been subject to earthquakes. On the 1st No- vember, 1755, a great shock occurred which overthrew almost all the pub- lic buildings and thousands of private houses. It is said that 30,000 people perished either in the ruins of the city, or in the attempt to save themselves by rushing on board the ships in the harbor. The greatest attraction here, to me, after the people, streets, houses, shops and public gardens, was the Church of St. Roch, with its world renowned Chapel of St. John. I remember of reading of this, years ago, and my first impulse, after getting rid of the Custom House formalities, and locating at the hotel, was to see this church. The exterior is plain, but the interior is very fine. I can give no better description of it than that I translate for you, which is correct.

"A brief description of the Royal Chapel of St. John the Baptist, made at Rome, by order of D. John V. of Portugal, and erected in the Church of St. Roch. The mosaic in the center is a representation of the Baptism of Christ in the Jordan; that on the right represents the An- nunciation of the Blessed Virgin Mary, and the one on the left, the De- scent of the Holy Ghost. These pieces are imitations, in mosaic, of the paintings of eminent artists; the Baptism of Christ being taken from Michael Angelo; the Annunciation from Guido, and the Descent of the Holy Ghost from Raphael. Fifteen years were spent in the execution of these mosaics by the ablest artists of the day. In the centre of the floor, which is also mosaic, is represented a globe, as if to indicate that the above mentioned pieces are the most famous in the world. The two panels on the ceiling, in Carrara marble, were executed under the direction of the renowned sculptor, Mayne Giusti, who brought the chapel to Portugal.

" There are in this chapel eight columns of lapis-lazuli. The other stones of which it is composed, are cornelian, amethyst, Egyptian alabaster, verde antique, Roman marble, and porphyry. The doors are bronze, beautifully worked, and gilt. The candelabra and the lamps are of solid silver, and the altar is ornamented with a scriptural group in *alto relievo*, which is one entire block of silver.

" In 1774 this chapel was temporarily set up in St. Peters, at Rome, for exhibition, and was consecrated by Benedict XIV, who said the first mass in it, after which it was taken down and conveyed to Portugal, where, in 1746, it was erected in the church of St. Roch,"—and here I found it. There were seven other chapels in the church, all ornamented with splendid paintings.

In the evening I went to the Opera, at the *Teatro Don Carlos 2d*, the second largest Opera House in Europe. The play was "Faust," and, certainly, if perfect singing, acting and scenic representation could define the thought of the author, and entrance the hearer in any play, it was done in this one. I sat near the orchestra, and had a good view of the six tiers of boxes that went upwards in gilded succession to the top, all full of Senors and Senoritas. The orchestra was composed of sixty-one performers, (my companion counted them,) mostly violinists, and at one time there were over two hundred ballet dancers on the stage together. Many of the officers of the United States Steamship Canandaigua were with us. She belongs to the Mediterranean Squadron, and had just come into port.

I had quite a long interview with our Minister, Hon. Jas. P. Harvey, who has been here for five years. He gave me a history of the trouble with the Stonewall and Niagara while they were here in port together. We visited the celebrated acqueduct and reservoir, called on the Spanish Minister, and admired the public gardens, streets, and pretty women, and so, *done* Lisbon.

Our party left on the train for Badajoz in Spain, at 7 A. M. on the morning of the 2d of January. Besides myself and my companion, Mr. G., there was a New Yorker who had been in the South American Republics for the past fourteen months, and whom we met in Brazil, and who had traveled over Asia Minor, Turkey, Russia, and through all the cities of Europe, except those of Spain, and also a Grecian gentleman and his wife, making five in all. The Greek was going to Smyrna, via Madrid and Marseilles. It has been my good fortune to meet with several Greek merchants, and I have found them uniformly well bred, highly cultivated, and intelligent upon every subject. They remind you of the Jew in their money getting proclivities, of the Yankee in their perseverance, and of the student and traveler in their culture. We five had an apartment in a car to ourselves. The route is almost due east, from Lisbon directly across Portugal. In the first eighty miles we went through a highly cultivated country, with orange, fig, and olive trees in abundance. The olive were as numerous as the coffee trees in Brazil. There were long rows of thousands of them. As we ascended to the upper plains, we found the cork tree almost universal. No other tree was to be seen for a hundred miles. The cork forests remind you of a great apple orchard, the trees being the same size, and just about as far apart. There is no undergrowth, and no other cultivation except the grape, and now and then a wheat field. The exportation of cork must be very great. I saw piles of it at several of the railway stations, and vessels laden with it in the harbor of Lisbon.

We passed through several towns on our route, among others, Santeram, founded in 406 by the Romans, and afterwards occupied by the Moors. Near this place, on an island in the river, seemingly made on purpose to hold it, there is an entire Moorish castle, with donjon, keep and battlement, in perfect condition, as it stood a dozen centuries ago. As we swept along, every line of it was clearly defined in the declining sunlight·

I had expected to find very mountainous regions in the east of Portugal, but, on the contrary, although high, the country was a level plain, with now and then an elevation upon which was perched a walled city, with its garden fringes. There are no natural Pyrenees, no deep Tagus, or any Chinese wall that divides these two kingdoms. A small rivulet, the *Caya*, is the rubicon, and parts those who speak the sonorous Castilian from the squeaking Lusitanian.

> "And scarce a name distinguisheth the brook.
> Though rival kingdoms press its verdant sides,"

says Byron, in Childe Harold, of this very stream.

"Elvas" is the last town on the Portuguese frontier. It is quite celebrated in history. It is strongly fortified and contains an arsenal, a canon foundry, a manufactory of arms, extensive barracks, and a theatre. It has about 10,000 inhabitants. It has been subject to a great many reverses in the wars of the centuries that have passed over it. We crossed the "Caya" at sundown and came to Badajoz, five miles from the frontier of Portugal. Here our baggage was examined, and we changed cars for Merida, thirty miles distant.

Badajoz is an important frontier place, and owes its interest to military events. It was taken from the Moors in 1235. Kellerman and Victor failed before it in 1808. It was the scene of many of Wellington's battles during the war of the Peniusula. The arms of Badajoz are the pillars of Hercules, and the motto, *Plus Ultra.* This *beyond*, has yet to be accomplished, so I think, after a look at it.

We arrived at Merida, where we take the diligencia at 8 P. M.

H. S. S.

No. 9.

MERIDA—ANCIENT TOWN--MOORISH ANTIQUITIES—A DILIGENCE RIDE—ENTERING MADRID--A SPANISH HINT TO CLEVELAND.

MADRID, Jan. 6, 1866.

At Merida we had a decided set-back,—quite a disappointment. The diligencia was full. We had been told at Lisbon, by the American Minister, who had recently passed over the route to Paris and back, that there was no necessity for telegraphing in advance for seats in the diligence ; that the revolutionary troubles in Spain had stopped travel, and there would be plenty of room. So others told us, and, we, strangers to the land, were taken in at Merida for twenty-four hours. However, we found, although time was of account, that we had stumbled upon something worth staying for, and I will proceed to tell you what it was, in the best language I know of out of Spain.

We got our luggage up to the little Fonda called the "*Posada de los Diligencia*"—stage inn—an exact description of which you will find in Don Quixote, and were standing around, grumbling at each other and everything, waiting for some beds to be put up for us, when it occurred to me that I had somewhere read of the Moorish and Roman ruins at this place ; and, on inquiry, found out that we should see something that would repay us for the delay and trouble ; so we went to bed, for the first time in Spain, and in tolerable good humor. The next morning I took my first good look at old Spain. It is hard to analyze one's impressions where there is so much novelty in every thing. My mind reverted at once to the old times, away down the centuries, before the Christian despoiler came to mar the glorious works of art left by the Moors, and, yet farther.

through the dark ages, when the Visigoths ruled the fair land, and still beyond, to the time, centuries before Christ, when the Phœnicians, and afterwards the Carthagenians, and still subsequently the Romans held sway. The Romans were invited over, about two hundred years before Christ, by the inhabitants of the country, to protect them from their neighbors; and, I suppose, liking the land, they quietly appropriated it to themselves—a little business transaction which has found its imitators even to the present day. But, in the sweep of the centuries, came the Retribution, and the doctrine of compensation was fully vindicated, when, after seven hundred years of quiet.luxurious occupation, the Visigoths poured down from the northern plains, and, in their turn, enjoyed the magnificent *vegas* and fruitful soil. History was renewed again when the Moors came from Africa and drove away the Goths. It was some five hundred years before the last strong hold of the Moors was taken by the Christians. But give me the pagans, or the Got hs--for theyre spected the Roman remains—or the Moors, with their knowledge of the arts, in preference to the race that now inhabit this land, Look at this place, Merida. Under the Romans it was the capital of Lusitania, and counted seven hundred thousand inhabitants. Its walls extended twentyone miles. The vast level plains that surround it, are full of the ruins of a great city. The little miserable pinched up town now, has about four thousand lazy, indolent people, whose peculiarities are not worth describing. According to an inscription I found on a monument, a tall marble shaft with a carved figure upon it, the city was founded by Augustus, for the settlement of his veteran troops, the Emirita. We visited Saint Eulalia, a huge convent—the Aleazar, partly Roman and partly Moorish. This old palace and castle overlooks the river Guadiana, and is very interesting. The owner of the place has built him a house in the enclosure, and has some of the finest orange and lemon groves I have yet seen. In it is also a church, formerly a Roman temple, afterwards a Moorish mosque, and now a place for Christian worship. The evidences of the Roman and Moorish architecture are abundant in this building, and also in the baths near by, where the Roman arches, in the descent we made of sixty-one steps, are perfect, but were so improved upon by the Moorish arabesques, that it is difficult, at first, to determine upon tho origin. It is this combination of the two eras of art that give to this portion of Spain, its superiority over every other place which the art seeker and the antiquarian love to visit. Merida has been called the Rome of Spain, but with all due deference to the vast ruins in Rome, there must be that lack of Moorish combination, which is only found here. I account for the preservation of these remains, from the fact, that here, on the confines of Spain and Portugal, away from any travel until within the past year a railroad has been completed, the vandals have not had an opportunity to quarry them away. The Government has, however, been lately taking a zealous interest in the preservation of many of the ruins. As, for instance, just near the railroad depot are some splendid arches, the remains of an aqueduct built by the Emperor Trajan twenty centuries ago. The engineer laid his road directly through one of these, but the government stopped it, and the road was obliged to diverge a little. The most interesting place to me was the fine Roman bridge which crosses the Guardiana, of eighty-one arches, and 2,500 feet in length. I spent some hours in the bright day upon and under the arches. I should think it would be of peculiar interest to the antiquarian, the historian and the architect. I afterwards went out upon the plains a mile or so, to see the old Roman circus and theatre. These were formerly in the centre of the city. About half of the vast amphitheatre is almost intact. The walls at the base, at the several entrances, are thirty-six feet through, and the arches are perfect. The upper walls are made of concrete, which has crumbled in places. The seats are all there, in stone, as when first laid by the builder. Within the present city limits there is an arch built by Trajan, sixty feet high by forty broad. The huge cut stones are slightly rounded by the wear and tear of ages, but will hold up for many more to come.

So much for Merida, which I would advise every traveler who comes this way to visit.

Next in order comes our diligence ride of forty hours, one hundred and three leagues, to Madrid, through a most interesting portion of Spain. We had taken the precaution to get the best seats, and except for the cramped up places, we got along very well, varying the monotony by walking up some of the hills.

The eight mules are hitched to the huge stage coach, four abreast, and are kept on a run over all the roads on the plains. They are changed frequently. The first important town we came to was Truxillo. It stands on he declivity of a granite hill, crowned by an ancient castle, and has an imposing appearance. Here Pizarro, the conqueror of Peru, was born, and he lies buried in the Church near the Fonda where we stopped. The next place of any importance is Talavera. It is beautifully situated on the right bank of the Tagus, which is here crossed by a bridge of thirty or forty arches, built in the Fifteenth Century. Here, in July, 1809, was fought the battle in which the English and Spanish troops, under the Duke of Wellington, defeated the French under Joseph Bonaparte, and Marshals Jourdain and Victor. There are some Roman remains, and the plains are covered with Moorish towers.

We then came to Maqueda and Naralcarnero. The country is, generally speaking, uncultivated, except in the vicinity of the towns and villages, and exhibits, to the left, a long chain of iron covered mountains. Everything on the plains is green and growing, and the weather very much as it is with us in June. From the elevation on which was perched the last station, twelve miles, we could see the long line of buildings which distinguish Madrid from the dry, arid plains which everywhere surround it. It was Sunday afternoon, and the people were out in the suburbs pic-nicking, and happy looking enough. We entered the city by the gate of *Foncarral*, and our route led directly by two fronts of the palace into the "Calle Alcala." Here we stopped in the *Puerto del Sol,*—opening for the Sun—at the "Hotel of the Princes." This *Puerto* is a square, about as large as ours in Cleveland, with a statue and fountains in the center. It is paved all over, and surrounded with hotels, cafes, all kinds of goods, the Post Office and other public buildings. There is splendid stores of no ugly looking wooden fence, or any obstruction whatever to a free travel all over it. The trees and foliage, instead of being placed in the principal business street, are found in profusion in the Prado and Public Gardens, where they should be to be appreciated. The people in all the Catholic Countries I have visited, with all their faults, are far ahead of us in this provision for the public. New York has seen the importance of these improvements in creating the Central Park. Cleveland might do something by locating a Prado upon the Lake shore, and relieving Superior Street of its present incubus. It will be done sometime.

What I have seen in Madrid in my limited time, and without the assistance of an Asmodeus to uncover the roofs of the houses, I shall try to tell you about in a day or two.   H. S. S.

No. 10.

MADRID TO GRENADA—THE PROVINCE OF LA MANCHA—
SCENES OF DON QUIXOTE'S EXPLOITS—GRENADA—THE
ALHAMBRA—A GIPSY DANCE—THE OPERA—THE CA-
THEDRAL—TOMBS OF FERDINAND AND ISABELLA.

GRENADA, Spain, Feb. 10, 1866.

I came from Madrid to Grenada, by rail to Almuradill, about one hundred and seventy-five miles, thence by diligence one hundred and twenty
miles, through Baylen, Jaen, and some other towns. The whole time
was thirty hours. We left Madrid at nine in the evening, and came to
the station where we took our stage—or diligencia—at daylight. This
coach is unique in its apartments and appointments, but, I should think,
well calculated for a trip over the mountains of Grenada. It has the
coupe, above, for four persons; the *berlina*, below, in front, for three, and
the *interieure*, also below and in the rear, for six. The baggage, on top,
behind the *coupe*. For the first thirty miles we passed over a level,
dreary country, nearly flat, with now and then a town, where we exchan-
ged mules. We had ten mules at each change, two abreast, with a pos-
tillion on one of the leaders. These were all kept on a full run the whole
way; up and down, and through everything, the same yell was heard
from driver and guard, keeping up a gallop without a stop. Fortunately
the roads were good—as are all the roads I have yet seen in Spain—and
we made good time.

We passed through Manzanares, memorable for the scene of Don
Quixote's knighthood. The road, made by Charles III nearly a century
ago, winds through a mountain gorge, with toppling crags above and
around, some of which are called here *los organos*, from representing the
pipes of an enormous organ. The province of La Mancha, which we now
enter, is mostly table land, and about two thousand feet above the sea.
It is entirely denuded of trees, and except occasionally, where, in the
dips of the undulating plains, a streamlet creates a partial verdure and
fertility, there is a great want of water. We get tired with the wide expanse of monotonous steppes. Nothing but the genius of a Cervantes
could have thrown any charm over its dullness. The towns are poor,
and without a particle of comfort or interest. The whole country was

so overrun during the war of the Peninsula, that nothing seems to have been left. The peasants of the country seem quiet, patient, and honest enough. With their picturesque *serapias*, and brown cloth clothes, they look the very image of Sancho Panza—the homely, real, Manchegan peasant. He is the true *Juan Espanol*—the simple John Bull of Spain. After passing through the gorge, we think of Don Quixote, Cardenia, and Dorethea, as realities. Among the mountains to the left was the scene of the knight's penance. Somewhere near there he liberated the gallant slaves. This is Don Quixote's country, and everybody who passes through it should have his story with him.

All along the route, through La Mancha, we imagined the Hidalgo, tall, spare and punctilious, balanced by the short, round, fat and familiar squire, in his *pano pardo*, greedy, beggarly and somnolescent. You may see plenty of them whenever the diligence stops. It is heresy to read Don Quixote except in his own language. It is like some one says of Schelegel's translating Shakespeare—transferring English gold into German Silver. One word here for honest Sancho Panca's proverbs—*Refraues*, they call them—which are peculiarly classical, Oriental and Spanish. These wise saws and maxims are in the mouths of every Sancho I have met in the Peninsula. They seem to be the burden of their song and speech. A proverb, well introduced, is as decisive of an argument as a bet is with us. This shotting a discourse has settled my questions with them sometimes to my own discomfort. I would advise travelers in this country never to get angry. It does no good. They meet you, if you are in a hurry, which you always are, with a shrug and *Paci-enza Senor, espera poco*—have patience, sir, and wait a little.

The next town we come to is Santa Cruz de Mudilla, a dull place of about 5,000 inhabitants. The women here offer garters for sale, with all sorts of embroidered mottos, quite untranslatable.

" *Te digan estas ligas,*
Mis penas y fatigas,"

Feliz quien los aparta, and so forth. Some of these Epigrammata are truly antique. You can compare them with the inscription on the girdle of Hermione. The city of Jaen, with about 12,000 inhabitants, stands at the entrance of the mountain passes of Grenada. You can see it from the plains as you approach, lying at the foot of the huge mountain, with the ruins of the castle just above it. The road for miles is straight, with a gentle rise, wide, smooth and lined with shade trees. As we approached, in the afternoon, the people were out in their best attire, as it was, as usual, a holiday with them. We changed our ten mules for as many others, and then went through the gorges of the mountains. Here is where the Moors defeated the great army sent out from Seville, in the glorious style described by Irving, when the stately and heroic warriors with which the whole stage glitters in this drama, were overpowered by the rocks from the toppling crags thrown down from above by the Moors. The mountain scenery is very grand, the villages on the way, old, decaying and quiet. Olives, grapes, figs and pomegranites grow in abundance. The aloe and the cactus is also frequently seen.

I arose early in the morning in Grenada, for a walk, and a visit to the barber's. Here you find the old Don's identical helmet, as you do all over Southern Spain, suspended immediately in front over the door, instead of the striped pole. It is a bright wash basin, of brass, with a wide rim, and the crescent like cut, out of one side. The city of Grenada has about 60,000 inhabitants, with some people of as much refinement, hospitality and good appearance as I have found in Spain. You know its location. The old Moorish part, the *Albaycin* of that time, on the declivity of the hill going down to the meeting of the Darro with its bride, the Xenil, and the later built portion below, which surrounds both this hill, and partially the Alhambra. The fortress of the Alhambra covers the curvatures of the mountain on which it stands, and seems to have been constructed with reference to it; so that, while its length is about three-fourths of a mile, it breadth varies from five hundred to one thousand feet. I entered through the long groves that you have read of, by the nearest gate, which is to the left. This old Moorish gate and archway has been so often described that I shall not attempt a description of it, nor of anything else except simply my own impressions of the place. Upon reaching the plateau above, we found the gardens and unfinished palace of Charles the Fifth, standing as when he left it. The walls splendidly ornamented, are about forty feet high, windowless and roofless In the interior is a circular court surrounded by galleries. To the left of this building we proceed into the Palace of the Alhambra, and first find ourselves in the Court of Myrtles. This is an oblong space surrounded by arches and pillars, all exquisitely ornamented with arabesques. The line of myrtles overlook the long bathing pool in the centre. From this we proceed to the Court of Lions, so called from the large fountain in its centre being supported by ten or twelve stone lions. The pillars, one hundred and twenty-four in number, and galleries, are wonderful. At the right you enter the hall of Martyrs, and immediately opposite, the *dos Hermanas*, the hall of the Two Sisters, so called from the two large and perfectly pure white marble slabs in the floor directly under the dome. This is the gem of the whole place, from the fact that it has been restored from the vandalism of the earlier Christians, and now stands out in its beauty and gracefulness, giving a complete idea of how splendidly the old Moorish sultans lived, and how much they must have regretted its loss. No wonder they fought two hundred years for its possession. Since Irving's time, the government have gone to work in an enlightened and vigorous way, and have the whole place now in perfect order and cleanliness, and have employed some fine artists to restore the whole of the ornamentations, arabesques and the original discriptions. The honey-comb stalactical pendants in the cealings have been retouched by the pencil, and you have all the Moorish colors, gold, (yellow) red and blue. These conical ceilings, which are common all over the Alhambra, are capable of an infinite variety of combinations, and attest the wonderful power and effect obtained by the repetition of the most simple elements. The artist informed me that over five thousand pieces entered into the construction of the ceiling of *Las dos Hermanas* alone. I visited the Hall of the Ambassadors; the Sultana's bed chamber looked down upon the garden, the *Lendaraja*, so beautiful once. I spent seven short hours in the place. I waited behind the others to admire again the elegant architecture of the galeries, and the slim columns, which appear unequal to the superincumbent weight. The thin pillars, and gossamer perforated fabric, looked like fairy work. The masses above seem to hang in the air instead of being supported from below. Few airy castles of illusion will stand the prosaic test of reality, and nowhere less than in Spain, as I thought when I in vain tried to discover the famous *Chateaux d' Espagne* as I passed along and across the *Guadalquiver* in coming here, but in the Alhambra, when the declining sunlight tips, with its semi-obscure, the filligree arches, a depth is given to the shadows, and a misty undefined magnitude to the saloons beyond, which surrenders you, for the time, to the past, and to the Moor. I looked from its high tower over and across the Vega which is twenty by seventy miles in length. On the left is the Sierra, covered with snow ; opposite, and to the left, is the old city of Albaycin ; below, the city of Grenada, and in front the splendid plains, enclosed by distant mountains, covered with white villages and olive groves. It is something to have seen two of the three great sights or views of the world—the Bay of Rio de Janeiro and the Vega of Grenada—in so short a time. We visited also the *Generalief*, the summer palace of the Moorish kings, which is in good repair and surrounded with gardens. It stands behind and above the Alhambra, and has so many objects of interest in and about it, that I cannot find a good place wherein to commence a description, and must therefore not attempt it.

We had sent down to one of the Gipsy villages on the Vega, where they live among the cactus, olives and aloes, to have some of their dancers come up in the evening, and after dinner we went to see them. The Chief came up and brought six *Gitanos* with him, who danced the *olio*, *bolero*, and many of their own dances, to the music of the guitar, for an hour, and then we went to the opera. We found it filled with the *elite* and fashion of the city of Grenada. A dancer, very celebrated here in the south of Spain, led the ballet troupe, and I have rarely seen them equalled, never in our own country. The audience were of as much interest to me as the players. The women of Grenada, as well as those of Madrid, are celebrated for their beauty and gracefulness, and here I saw some types of female beauty that will compare with any I have ever seen. The men were fine looking, well dressed and quite polite.

This morning we spent at the Cathedral, where we found some fine paintings, and also the tombs of Ferdinand and Isabella. These are in one of the Chapels of the vast Church. It has a rich gothic portal, wrought with many heraldic emblems. On two magnificent sepulchres, in the centre of the chapel, are extended the marble figures of these Catholic Sovereigns. Ferdinand and Isabella slumber side by side, life's fitful fever over, in the peaceful attitude of their long and happy union. The statue of Isabella is perfect in its carving. Her smile is as cold, and her look is as placid as moonlight sleeping on snow. She died, so history states, far from Grenada, but desired to be buried here. We next went to the convent of the Carthusians, about two miles from the city, but I cannot now tell you of the splendid sacristy, with its two paintings by Murillo, surrounded by precious stones, of the huge doors inlaid with tortoise-shell, ivory and pearl, of the two immense agates near the altar, a foot and a half each in diameter, and so on, for my candle is out.

H. S. S.

No. 11.

IN MADRID—THE AMERICAN CONSULATE—CARNIVAL WEEK—THE ESCURIAL—ITS MANY WONDERS—THE PAINTINGS BY THE OLD MASTERS.

MADRID, Feb. 14, 1866.

I am fortunate in being in Spain during the carnival week. There are no Americans here except two families, and our Minister and suite. I understand that the Boulevards in Paris are cleared of our countrymen now, as they have gone to Rome to see the sights there. If I have an opportunity I will give you a sketch of the three days carnival here. Whatever may be seen in Rome, I doubt if it exceeds that in Madrid. The people here—gay, indolent, fond of amusement and show—are all let loose on these days, and the mummeries and masquerades are as extravagant as I wish to see. It is strange to me that none of our people abroad visit Spain. They all go the stereotyped guide book track, through England to Paris, Germany and Rome, and they think they have "gone and done it." This may be accounted for in part from the fact that, until recently, there has been no through railroad from Paris, and the reputation of the roads, on account of robbers, is bad. The frequent revolutions—creating a discontented populace and soldiery—the lack of knowledge of the language, and the indisposition to leave the beaten track, which they must "do" at all events, have been controlling reasons also. But to me, this country has always been of peculiar interest, ever since I was old enough to read the Chronicles of the Cid, the tales of the Alhambra, Gil Blas and Don Quixote.

My introduction to our Legation, was, for some reason, very favorable, and I am indebted to our Minister, Hon. John P. Hale, and his family, for two or three pleasant evenings and for many courtesies. They are stopping at the same hotel for the present. The office of the Legation is in the *Calle Alcala*. Here, for about fourteen years, Horatio N. Perry, Esq., Secretary of Legation, has served our country well. To him and his amiable wife, a Spanish lady, I am under a thousand obligations.

Besides the trip to Grenada, Cordova, Seville, and the south of Spain generally, there are the city of Toledo, and the sights in this city, all of surpassing interest. I visited here the Congresis—the Cortes—now in session, and listened to the exciting debates, occasioned by the recent attempts at revolution. Also the Royal Museum with its two thousand paintings, by Murillo, Guido, Raphael, Rubens, Claude Lorain, Michael Angelo, and many others; its wonderful mosaics and sculpture, and other works of art. The collection of armory in the old palace is said to be unsurpassed in the world. Here is the armor of the Cid, of Columbus, of Ferdinand, and also of Queen Isabella, which she wore in the campaign against the Moors in Grenada; also that of Boabdil the last King of the Moors, and other Moorish armor; scimitars, ancient guns, pistols, lances, banners, jeweled crowns and ornaments without number. These are all arranged in well lighted galleries, numbered and catalogued.

I have made it a specialty to visit the cathedrals and convents, as far as practicable, in all the places I have been, but, as I am not writing a book, I can give but a slight glimpse of any of them in this place, and many must be left out altogether. They are open all day, and you can tread lightly around among the scattered worshippers, kneeling upon the pavement, without question. (And just here, in parenthesis, let me say by way of explanation, that in a former letter from Brazil, speaking of the accessibility to the Catholic Churches, I may have omitted to give credit to Doctor Ford's book for a paragraph. I find I have done so in looking over my notes, a copy of which I sent you.) Upon application to the Sacristan he will send an attendant, with huge keys, to open the *Costodias Sacristias*, chapels, &c., who will give all the required information. There is no fee, but you are expected to give the attendant a shilling or two for "the poor."

Among other instances of the moral and intellectual bondage of the people here, is one which is an epitome of itself. In the Cathedral at Grenada there is upon several of the huge pillars the following printed notice: " *Nadie se passce hable con Mujeres in este en Corrillos Enestas naves per de Excommunicacion y dos ducados para abras pias se.*, which means, that if any man speaks to a woman in any part of the Church he shall be excommunicated unless he pays two dollars! My friend thought it was cheap enough for the privilege of speaking to some of the very pretty *Granadalinos* we had seen in the churches, streets, and at the opera.

There is one place, however, of which I will give you my impressions, at the risk of wearying the reader. The *Escurial*—the burial place of the Kings and Queens of Spain for centuries—is the greatest sight of the kind I have yet seen, and which no one can visit without wonder, and without some expansion of the mind.

In the immense palace of the *Escurial*, a whole day will only afford a hurried visit. The stupendous edifice of the Monastery, a mountain of granite shaped into a palace, can hardly be seen in so short a time. You should make several visits to it to look out of each of its four thousand windows. It is about thirty miles (one hour and a half by rail) from Madrid, and a half league from the station. Its characteristics, as they seemed to me, are vast proportions, admirable harmony and unity of design, simplicity, massiveness and grandeur. The different races who settled here in turn—the Romans, Goths and Arabs—were all builders, each after their own peculiar style. The Christians seemed to have adopted some ideas from them all. Here are quarries of granite and beautiful marble; and, where the glorious light of the sun and stars give such relief to outlines, and depth to shadows, and brightness of tints, splendid edifices of all kinds would seem likely to abound. I will translate for you a description of the Escurial, which I have also condensed somewhat. " This palace was designed by Phillip II, and the first stone was laid in April, 1563, and was completed in 1586, twenty-one years after, at a cost of $3,300,000. The edifice itself, that is, without the offices, is a paralellogram, seven hundred and forty-four feet long by five hundred and eighty broad. It is of the Doric order, and made entirely from the marble and granite of the quarries in the vicinity. From its angles and centre spring eight towers, about two hundred feet high, and crowned by the cupola of the church. Every thing in the edifice is on a colossal scale. Suffice it to state, that there are sixteen courts, forty altars, one thousand two hundred doors, eighty-six staircases, three thousand feet of fresco painting, eighty-nine fountains, etc. The church, inside, is all granite, three hundred and twenty feet long. The form resembles a Greek Cross. The pulpits are made of alabaster, and the richest marbles, ornamented with medallions. The altar stands isolated, and is made of marbles and inlaid jasper, with a jasper stone of one whole piece." And so I might go on until you got as tired out as I was. The multitude of paintings, and the excessive ornamentation become wearisome, after a time. The pictures in the *retablo*, which is about one hundred feet high and composed of red granite and jasper, deserve close inspection. The guide said there were about seven hundred relics, among which are ten whole bodies, one hundred and fifty heads, and about double that number of whole arms and legs. On the right of the altar, in the *oratorio*, are five statues, those of Charles V, the Empress Isabella, Phillip II, Phillip III, and the Queen Maria. These are said to be portraits, and are very remarkable for their execution, especially in the details of the embroidery. In the *Sacristia* are very many fine paintings :—Jacob watching Labans flock, by Ribera ; a Transfiguration, by Raphael ; Christ washing the Apostles' feet, by Tintoretto. This last picture was painted for Charles I, of England, but was afterwards purchased by Phillip IV, of Spain. No. 81 on the catalogue is Jesus bearing the Cross, by Guido, and 88 a Crucifixion, by Titian, both wonderful. These you must see when you come here, and also No. 84, a large painting by Claudio, who, after seven years labor, made it his masterpiece. The subject is the ceremony which took place in this very sacristia in the presence of Charles II. All the heads are portraits. It is a very fine large picture, full of expressiveness from its numerous figures, and forms a page of history worth volumes. You will find a copy of it in the Madrid picture gallery. You will see some specimens of fine embroidery, for which Spain has always been celebrated. There is one vestment embroidered after designs by El Mudo, which is said to be valued at £45,000.

The *Camarin* was erected in 1692—so says the inscription. It stands in one of the inside court yards. There is a glorious collection here of precious marbles, which must certainly be unrivalled, There is a *custodia* containing above ten thousand precious stones—quite tiresome to look at without the privilege of handling. There is a fine old folio, written by some ancient monk, containing about twenty beautiful miniatures, done up by the great miniaturists of the time, whose names are all there. In the *del coro*, or choir, are kept some collossal choral books, some of them six feet wide, each leaf made from the skin of a calf. The style of letter is singular—at least, to me. They are all magnificently illuminated. There is a little stall here, simple but elegant and well carved, made of ebony, cedar, box and other woods. The story on the inscription is that Phillip II, the founder, was here kneeling in prayer, when, through the small door to the left, a messenger glided in, bearing the news of the destruction of the Armada, in the English channel. "His countenance remained impassible, and he resumed his prayers." So says the Spanish chronicle. The gem of this choir is the beautiful Carrera marble crucifix. It was made by Cellini, and is labelled "Benvenutus Cellinus, 1562." The great Florentine carved it for the Duke of Tuscany, by whom it was presented to Phillip II. This, with a bit of curious autobiography, is worth translating. He says : " Although I have made several marble statues, I shall only mention one, from its being of a kind most difficult for art to render—that is, dead bodies. I speak of the image of our Lord crucified, for which I studied a great deal, working upon it with a diligence and love that so precious a *simulacre* deserves ; and also because I knew myself to be the first who ever executed crucifixes in marble." From the choir you descend a few marble steps and come iuto the *panteon*. These vaults were built at different periods, by Phillip II, III and IV. I don't like this place ; there is an icy blast of death, which, with the sombre darkness and ironical gilding of bones, seems oppressive amid the shining marbles. There is nothing of the feelings that fill the soul and mind in the presence of the truly christian and beautiful tombs in some of the Medieval Cathedrals I have visited, with their sculptured effigies, praying or asleep. This name of *Panteon* is pagan, although it was completed in 1654, according to the inscription. Over the portal is the history of its erection. "*Locus sacer mortalibus Exuviis,*" etc. At the sides are Roman allegorical statues. All around the octagonal chamber, which, I should think, was about forty feet high, and the same across it, are placed in rows, within nitches, a number of marble urns, identically sized, and not unlike an anatomical collection. The kings are placed on the right of the altar, for you must bear in mind that now you are in the *Escurial*, the burial place, as I said before, of the Kings and Queens of Spain for centuries. The Queens are on the left as you enter. There are wanting Ferdinand and Isabella, whose tombs and effigies I saw in Granada.

In the Convent you find some very fine pictures. One is, Noah intoxicated, by Giadano. The Satyrs, by the same, is very good. St. Marguerite, by Titian ; also, St. JeromePraying, and the Prayer on Olivet, by the same. Flowers by Bassano, originally belonging to Charles I, of England. A copy of Titian's Ecce Homo, by El Mudo.

The palace is placed in an angle of the edifice. The principal staircase is a wonder of art. The walls of the rooms we visited are hung with tapestry, many of which were made in Flanders, from designs by Teniers, and others from the Fabrica of Madrid. Phillip II's own room is almost a cell, very plain. There are but few remains of furniture dating of that time. In the *sala battallas*, so called from the frescoes on the wall representing great battles and sieges, one fresco dates 1587, and was copied, so it says, by order of Phillip, from a chiara-oscuro canvass some one hundred and thirty feet long, found in a lumber room in the Alcazar of Segovia. I should think it very important to artists, and others, on account of the costume, arms, and military disposition of troops in those times. There are rooms also in this building, richly ornamented with inlaid wood. Four of the rooms, created in Charles IV's time, are said to have cost £280,000. They are labelled *piezas de maderas finas.*" There are manypictures here—a Virgin by Cano, a view of Venice, and others by Velasquez, Giordan and Carracci.

In the *Casita del Principe* there are some good specimens of marquetry, and ivory work, worthy of Chinese patience, even ; jaspers and gilding, faded silks and furniture.

The view from the towers of the *Escurial* embraces extensive but melancholy wastes, with a railroad running close by this monument of by-gone ages, in whose cold granite bosom sleep the mighty representatives of the genius, power, grandeur and backwardness of their age. It is the grandest and gloomiest place I have yet seen.

H. S. S.

No. 12.

A LAST LOOK AT MADRID—THE ROYAL STABLES—THE PICTURE GALLERIES—THE MUSEUM—THE PRADO— MADRID TO PARIS—THE FRENCH CAPITAL—LONDON— COMING HOME.

LONDON, Feb. 20, 1866.

Before leaving Madrid I went to the old buildings of the Inquisition. They have no particular outside appearance differing from thousands of other old buildings in the city. As I stood in the dungeons, where so much suffering had been caused by the spirit of error, I could not help thinking how much of the animus of the Inquisition still lives among the bigoted of all nations, and especially here, where no Cortes or Constitution ever permits any approach to religious toleration. I am told that many here believe, that in the changes and chances of Spain it may be re-established; hence you will find no one who will converse with you on the subject; sons of burnt fathers, they dread the fire.

The stranger, in going about Madrid for the first time, should take a *lacquai de place*, or guide, as many places, and especially the chief lions, can only be visited on certain days, and at certain hours. There is a class of guides here, called Rock-Scorpions—Gibraltar bred Spaniards —who speak English. I had one at Grenada, and found him thoroughly well posted and very useful. You need them but once, as you soon get posted yourself. I visited the Royal Stables, with their three hundred and twenty horses and two hundred and forty mules; there are some of the finest breeds of horses in the world here. The Andalusian breed is celebrated. I have seen a better average class of horses in Spain than in any other country I have been in. In these stables are some Arabian mares of great beauty, also some English mares, some minute ponies belonging to the little Prince of the Asturias, and a great variety of mules. The Royal carriages, about one hundred and twenty-five in number, are ranged along side by side in an extensive building. Here are some state carriages dating three hundred years back, and so along, showing all the different fashions and improvements to the present time; they were, most of them, made either in France or England, and are all very elaborately ornamented with tortoise shell panels, gold, ivory and pearl. On opening them I saw some beautiful specimens of embroidery, with linings of cloth of silver and gold.

I made one more visit to the Royal Museum, to see, especially, two or three paintings—one, the Transfiguration, by Murillo, and two by Claude Lorraine. The first had haunted me ever since I first saw it; it does so now, and always will. Ford says, in his description of this Museum : "To give a general idea of the extraordinary contents of this, the finest gallery in the world, suffice it to say, that there are twenty-five Bassanos, ten Claudes, twenty-two Vandyks, sixteen Guidos, forty-six by Murillo, ten by Raphael, fifty-three by Ribera, sixty-two by Rubens, fifty-two by Teniers, forty-three by Titian, twenty-seven by Tintoretto, sixty-two by Velasquez, twenty-four by Paul Veronese, fourteen by Zurbaran, and several hundreds by the other eminent artists of their day. No collection of pictures was ever begun or continued under greater advantage. Charles V and Phillip II, both real patrons of art, were the leading sovereigns of Europe during the bright period of the *Renaissance*, when fine art was an every day necessity, and pervaded every relation of life. Again Phillip IV ruled at Naples and in the Low Countries, at the second restoration of art, which he truly loved for itself. These three great Monarchs, like Alexander the Great, took a pleasure in raising their painters to personal intimacy; and nowhere have artists been more highly honored than Titian, Velasquez and Rubens were in the Palace of Madrid. At a later period, Phillip V, grandson of Louis XIV, added many pictures by the principal French artists of their Augustan age."

Not much can be seen in the short time I devoted to it, but I have a well defined consciousness that I have seen something I shall always remember. As for giving you my " impressions," that is quite out of the question. I came as a pilgrim to this temple of High Art, and bowed low at its shrine, a simple worshipper, and I confess that no language of mine can describe what I felt. I can readily see why art is considered the handmaid of religion, and why, in all these countries, the altar is associated with all painting of a high class. In going through the crowded halls of this museum, filled with the mighty spirits of the past, passing those acres of canvass, it seems as if a year were too short to examine its contents; but soon, the masses begin to simplify themselves, and we select such as we like by instinct, as it were, and confine ourselves to them. Picture seeing is, however, very fatiguing, for one is standing all the while, and with the body, the mind is also at exercise, and is exhausted by admiration. The mosaics in this museum are strange and new to me. There are several lapis lazuli tables, one of which cost $90,000. The tops are laid in mosaic of various designs.

There is here, also, a superb collection of goldsmith work of the Fifteenth Century, of above a hundred cups, tazzas and exquisite jeweled plate, by Celini, D'Arphes, Beceriles and others. Among them, I noticed particularly a mermaid, with emerald tail, rising out of gold, studded with rubies, by Cellini, and a cup supported by a female. But I must be moving on, which, by the way, seems to have been the order of the day ever since I started from home. I visited the Convent of Atocha. In the chapel is the celebrated image of the Virgin, the patroness of Madrid, and the especial protectress of the royal family, who worship here every Saturday. Here the royal marriages take place, and, when a Queen is in the case, her wedding dress becomes a perquisite of this Virgin. The present Queen, Isabella II, was on her way to this shrine when she was stabbed by Merino, some years since. The dress, with the dagger hole in it, is there. There are numerous chronicles of the miracles wrought by this Virgin. One author gives thirty-three pages to them. It expelled a devil from a boy named Blas, (I wonder if it was Gil?) It gave speech to a dumb beggar, who then distinctly (and quite naturally) said "*Di me un cuarto*"—Give me a copper—and many others.

The *Prado*, or promenade, from three to six every afternoon, presents a gay appearance, and a very unique one to a stranger. It runs across the *Calle Alcala*, the Superior street of Madrid, is two miles in length, and two hundred feet wide. There are two parallel roads for drives, and three wide promenade walks. These walks and drives are separated by shade trees. Many of the principal, public buildings and dwellings, line it on either side. There are eight fountains with elaborate sculptured figures. Those of Neptune, Apollo and Cybele, are very fine, but these stony things count as nothing when compared to the living groups of all ages, color and costume, which walk and talk, oggle or nod, or sit and smoke, It is just the place to study costume and manners. Ninety-nine out of every hundred smoke, and little Murillo-like urchins run about with lighted rope ends or matches, crying out " *candela*," " *fuego*," on every side, while *Agnadores* follow the fire, like engines, offering fresh water.

During the carnival, which lasts four days, the usual custom is to commence the great procession of carriages at 3 P. M. This forms at the Queens Palace, and, passing through the city for about a mile, stretches along the *Prado*, in single file, and at a walk.

As the line passed down by the hotel the other day, I went out accompanied by a friend, who has lived here long, and we walked up and down the length of the Prado. It was crowded with maskers of all descriptions —some utterly indescribable.

The long procession of carriages just filled up the four mile circuit. Some of their occupants were in masks, and very many were not, Altogether there were several thousands out, and the scene was gay and odd enough.

We went to the opera at 8, and to the masquerade ball at 11 P. M. The latter is an "institution" here. I got tired, finally, and leaving my companions went back to the hotel.

In this brief sketch I give but little of what I saw in Madrid. What I have to say of other places must be briefer still. We took leave of our kind friends—looked after our passports—packed up, with our trunks, many pleasant memories of the past few days—and took our tickets for Paris.

The distance from Madrid to Paris is nine hundred English miles—time forty hours. There are about seventy stations on the route. The first of any importance is Valladolid, the Roman Pincia, with its twenty thousand inhabitants. It is celebrated for many sieges and battles; also as the birth place of Phillip II, in 1527, and is the place where Columbus died in 1506. We pass through a portion of the province of Salamanca, through the cities of Burgos, Vittoria, Tolosa, and come to the Bay of Biscay at San Sebastiani, passing in the meantime through many tunnels and over heavy grades as we cross through the Pyrenees. The towns and cities have a tumbledown, non-improvement appearance. There are large fields of wheat and groves of fruit trees. The grape vine is everywhere and the olive tree spreads over the plains and along up the distant mountain sides in endless profusion. The forest trees have gone long ago ; fuel and timber for domestic purposes, therefore, are very dear.

From St. Sebastiani to Irun the time is about one hour. From Irun across the frontier into France, to Hidaye, just five minutes. Here we are in another world, almost. The houses, people, fields, everything, are changed in a moment, and we see the neat, trim peasantry, and the well cultivated fields and pretty flower-gardens of the south of France. The railroad all the way through is well built and managed. The first class cars are very comfortable, and luxuriously furnished. The *Buffets*, or dining places, are very good, and everything is neat and cleanly. We passed through Bayonne and Bordeaux, Tours and Orleans, to Paris, where we took our observations and our soup at the Grand Hotel, Boulevard Capucines. Every one knows all about Paris. To me it seemed a gay, white, light and bright city, in its general effect. The houses are principally composed of shutters and windows. The goods in the shops are tastefully and effectively laid out, and the *bonnes* on the benches wear such an amount of linen on their heads as would render them undistinguishable in a snow storm. The costumes of the women are, some pleasing, and some singular, and some of them both. The majority of them look like Little Red Riding Hood, with a difference of color. There is the Blue Riding Hood, the yellow, green and white, and sometimes the Black Satin Riding Hood, although she is at the Opera. Ladies past the age of thirty have evidently a strong passion for mustachios, for they wear them frequently on their own lips. The good folks upon the Boulevards walk slowly and chatter rapidly. Their conversation, not understanding it, reminds me considerably of seltzer water—it is so effervescent, vapid and colorless. They seem to pump it out of themselves with an action of the arm, very suggestive of the syphon.

The stranger cannot help noticing the immense improvements going on in Paris. Whole squares are taken down and rebuilt, and the streets are being widened and improved. Among other things, the old stone boulders have been taken up and Asphaltum pavement put in their place in most of the streets. The little joker who presides over the nation, after this was done, bending his nose slightly to meet the tip of his thumb, and waving his fingers gracefully in the soft air, says "My dear little children' we shan't have any more of those ugly barricades. Not any for me, *mon enfants*, if you please !"

I visited most of the places of interest here. Went to the churches of St. Germain-l'Auxerrois, Notre Dame, St. Eustache, Madelaine and others. I attended the opera, theatres, and other places of public amusements—looked in at *La Morgue*, the dead house, where three "unfortunates" who had been taken out of the Seine, were waiting for their friends to claim them. I spent a whole day in the gallery of the Louvre.

As there was not much more to be done, I left for London by the Calais and Dover route—time eleven hours. I met some friendly natives of ours, *en route*, and we have concluded to brave the storms of the March Atlantic together. If they are not too heavy, I shall be with you almost as soon as this letter. Here, I have been trying the underground railroad, looking into the Omnibus system, which is a good one, visiting churches, palaces, museums, operas, theatres, and other places, until I went (very naturally) to prison. Old Newgate has Jack Shepard's irons, also those of Dick Turpin, and many other relics of by-gone rascality, showing how little human nature changes with the centuries.

I might tell you much more about Paris and London, but I had rather send you a guide book with maps and illustrations, than attempt it, as my time is short and "I want to go home." I stop one day in Liverpool, and our steamer remains nearly a day at Cork, then for the Atlantic, Cape Race and New York harbor.   H. S. S.